RING ROUND THE MOON

ACTING EDITION

★

A CHARADE WITH MUSIC
BY JEAN ANOUILH
ADAPTED BY CHRISTOPHER FRY

★

DRAMATISTS
PLAY SERVICE
INC.

RING ROUND THE MOON was first presented at The Globe Theatre, London, on January 26, 1950.

The first American production was made by Gilbert Miller at the Martin Beck Theatre in New York City on November 23, 1950, with the following cast:

JOSHUA, a crumbling butler ....Francis Compton
HUGO, a young man about town ....Denholm Elliott
FREDERIC, his brother ....Denholm Elliott
   in love with
DIANA MESSERSCHMANN, engaged to Frederic ....Neva Patterson
LADY INDIA, Messerschmann's mistress ....Georgina Cookson
   secretly in love with **Hugo**
PATRICE BOMBELLES, Messerschmann's secretive
  secretary ....Michael Evans
MADAME DESMORTES, aunt to Hugo, Frederic
  and Lady India ....Lucile Watson
CAPULET, her faded companion ....Cynthia Latham
MESSERSCHMANN, Diana's father, a melancholy
  millionaire ....Oscar Karlweis
ROMAINVILLE, a patron of the arts ....Philip Tonge
   and of
ISABELLE, a ballet dancer ....Stella Andrew
HER MOTHER, a teacher of the pianoforte ....Brenda Forbes
A GENERAL ....Marcel Dill
FOOTMEN ....William Allyn
                                              Bennett Martin
(Double for Hugo/Frederic)

SYNOPSIS OF SCENES

The action of the play passes in a Winter Garden in Spring.

ACT I

SCENE 1. Morning.
SCENE 2. The same evening. Before the Ball.

ACT II

The same evening. The Ball.

ACT III

SCENE 1. The same evening. After Supper.
SCENE 2. Dawn.

RING ROUND THE MOON

ACT I

SCENE 1

SCENE: *A Winter Garden in Spring. Morning.*
A large, light framework structure representing the con-
servatory, occupies most of the stage, with sufficient
room for the acting area below it. Filling L. *side of*
conservatory is a rostrum with steps at upstage and
downstage ends. In R. *side a small mound with a palm-*
tree on it. A trellis-work screen stands below downstage
R. *corner of conservatory. Slender trellis-work wings* R.
provide exits D. R., R. C. *and* U. R. *Backstage a skycloth*
or cyclorama with a floral ground row. There are arbor
wings L. *with entrance* D. L. *which can be closed by*
jalousies, leading to ballroom. A wicker rocking-couch
stands R. C. *below conservatory.*
When curtain rises, HUGO, *a young man-about-town,*
enters D. R., *crosses to* C. *He is playing with a cup-and-*
ball. He is followed on by JOSHUA, *the butler, who*
stands D. R. *of couch.*

HUGO. And how about last night, Joshua? Did the same thing
happen?
JOSHUA. I'm sorry I can't deny it, Mr. Hugo, but the same thing
did.
HUGO. My brother slept all night under her window?
JOSHUA. Yes, Mr. Hugo—under both her windows. For five
nights now Mr. Frederic has gone to bed in a rhododendron bush:
you know, sir, the one on the south side of the west wing, beside
that statue they call Calliope, a classical character, sir. (HUGO
moves to L. *of* JOSHUA.) Every morning the housemaid has found
his bed unrumpled, and the gardener has found the rhododendron
bush rumpled. Well, it gives them a jolt, Mr. Hugo, as who
wouldn't it? I try to make light of it, so as to keep them in the

5

dark: but one day they'll talk and madam will know all about it.

HUGO. Have you ever been in love, Joshua?

JOSHUA. Now, sir, think: I've been in madam's service for thirty years; I'm too old.

HUGO. But before that?

JOSHUA. I was too young.

HUGO. (*Moving* U. C., *playing with his cup-and-ball*.) Mine's the age for it, Joshua. I fall in love as a matter of routine. But not ludicrously like my brother.

JOSHUA. No, sir. Mr. Frederic hasn't your style at all, sir.

HUGO. And yet we're the same age. It's odd, isn't it?

JOSHUA. You're ten minutes older, sir, remember that.

HUGO. Yes, I know. But who would have thought that those ten minutes would have taught me so much about women?

JOSHUA. (*Crossing above couch to* R. *of* HUGO.) The young lady knows she can do what she likes with your brother, sir.

HUGO. She may think she knows. But—I've schemed a scheme.

JOSHUA. I'm glad to hear that, Mr. Hugo.

HUGO. I got up early this morning because I've decided to take action. This dawn is the dawn of the unexpected. (*Moves* D. L. C.) What's the time?

JOSHUA. Twelve o'clock, Mr. Hugo.

HUGO. (*Backing to door* D. L.) By twelve-thirty, Joshua, I shall begin to loom big on the horizon. (*Exits* D. L.)

JOSHUA. (*Moving* D. L. C., *calling*.) Oh, and, Mr. Hugo, sir. (*Double steps into doorway* D. L. *and stands above downstage jalousie with his back to audience. He can be seen playing with a cup-and-ball held outstretched in his* L. *hand. While* JOSHUA *continues with his speech,* HUGO *passes around behind backcloth in readiness to make his entry* R. *as* FREDERIC.) I attempted to explain away the rhododendrons, sir, by informing the gardener that a wolf had been observed making depredations in the vicinity, sir. I told him not to mention this, sir, on the grounds that it might occasion the guests a measure of comprehensible alarm, sir. Thank you, sir. (*Double exits.* FREDERIC *enters* R. C., *moves to* R. *of couch*.)

FREDERIC. Joshua.

JOSHUA. (*Turning, moving* D. C.) Mr. Frederic?

FREDERIC. Has Miss Diana come down yet?

JOSHUA. Not yet, Mr. Frederic.

6

FREDERIC. (*Moving below couch.*) Do I look tired, Joshua?

JOSHUA. (*Moving* U. L. *of couch.*) If I may be allowed to be frank, yes, you do, sir.

FREDERIC. (*Sitting on couch.*) But you're quite mistaken, you know. I've never slept better.

JOSHUA. I think I should inform you, sir, the gardener intends to set wolf-traps in the rhododendrons.

FREDERIC. Never mind, Joshua. I'll sleep in the azaleas.

JOSHUA. (*Moving above couch to* R. *of it.*) And the housemaid, sir, the one who looks after the west wing, she has been making remarks of horrified dissatisfaction. She came to see me quite ready to drop. (*Starts to move* R.)

FREDERIC. Tell her, next time, to drop into my bed, if she would be so good, and untidy it herself.

JOSHUA. (*Turning, taken aback.*) Mr. Frederic!

FREDERIC. Why not? She's very charming. And when she's unmade it sufficiently she will be able to make it again, and everything will seem to be just as usual.

JOSHUA. Very good, Mr. Frederic. (*Exits* R. C. DIANA *enters* U. L., *goes up onto upstage end of rostrum.*)

FREDERIC. (*Rising, moving to* R. *of steps.*) Diana! How good to see you again. It's been like a lifetime since yesterday.

DIANA. (*Stopping midway on rostrum, looking at* FREDERIC.) Which one of you is it now?

FREDERIC. (*Reproachfully.*) Oh, Diana; that's not a nice thing to ask me.

DIANA. (*Moving and standing on top step.*) Ah, yes, it is you. You're looking at me like a little lost dog again. Did you get out of the wrong side of the rhododendrons? At first you looked so triumphant I thought you were your brother.

FREDERIC. If you prefer him to me, I shall go away and die.

DIANA. (*Patting* FREDERIC'S *cheek.*) Dear Frederic! You know I should only mistake you by accident. You're so alike.

FREDERIC. Our hearts aren't alike.

DIANA. No, that's true. (*Moves down steps.*) But imagine me alone in the park one evening: (*Crosses below* FREDERIC *to* R. C.) I hear the twigs cracking behind me and what sounds like your step: two arms go round me, and they feel like your arms: a mouth kisses me, and it feels like your mouth. How am I to have time to make sure it's the right heart, Frederic?

7

FREDERIC. (*A step towards her.*) But, Diana, I've never put my arms round you in the park.

DIANA. Are you sure?

FREDERIC. (*Moving to* L. *of her.*) Perfectly sure. Diana! It was my brother, looking like me on purpose. It was my double, double-crossing me again. I must find him: I've got to speak to him. (*He turns, starts to move* L.)

DIANA. (*Moving quickly to* R. *of* FREDERIC *and putting her hand on his arm, laughing.*) Now, dear, dear, dear, DEAR, DEAR Frederic! Don't go rushing to conclusions. I made it up. No one's been kissing me.

FREDERIC. (*Hanging his head.*) I beg your pardon, Diana. I completely believe you. But if Hugo loved you, I should kill myself.

DIANA. That would be terrible. I should never know which of you was dead. (*Pauses for a few moments as she moves on to bank and stands* R. *of tree.*) Of course it would be a great help to your brother; he would only have to drop a few tears for you at the funeral, and then come and whisper in my ear "Ssh! Don't tell anyone. They've made a great mistake. This is really Hugo's funeral." How should I answer that?

FREDERIC. (*Turning, moving* C.) But you couldn't be deceived for a moment, could you? If I were so exactly like Hugo, in word and thought and deed, I should *be* Hugo.

DIANA. Yes, that's true.

FREDERIC. (*After pause.*) Diana, it's Hugo you love. (*Turns and moves* L.) Good-bye.

DIANA. Are you mad? I hate him. Kiss me.

FREDERIC. (*Looking lost.*) Diana!

DIANA. Kiss me, you lost dog, and I'll find your way home for you.

FREDERIC. (*Moving below bank.*) I love you.

DIANA. (*Stepping off bank, moving in to* R. *of* FREDERIC.) I love you, too, Frederic. (*They kiss. She pushes* FREDERIC *away.*) I suppose you're quite sure you're not Hugo? He's capable of absolutely anything. (*She turns, moves* U. *through conservatory, exits* U. R. FREDERIC *follows her off.* LADY INDIA, *followed by* PATRICE BOMBELLES, *enters* D. R.)

PATRICE. (*As he enters.*) Anything! Anything! He's capable of absolutely anything.

LADY INDIA. (*Moving* C.) But, dear heart, how could he suspect us? We've been so careful.

PATRICE. I tell you, I wouldn't trust that fellow Hugo an inch. (LADY INDIA *turns, moves in to* L. *of* PATRICE. *He backs to* R.) Yesterday he giggled at me. Quite noticeably, as I went past him. (LADY INDIA *follows* PATRICE.) Why should he have giggled if he didn't know all about us?

LADY INDIA. (*Moving in close to* L. *of* PATRICE.) When did he giggle?

PATRICE. Last night, on the terrace, after dinner.

LADY INDIA. Last night? We were all there together. (*Turns, crosses to* L. C.) He choked himself with cigar-smoke. He was coughing.

PATRICE. (*Crossing and standing on bottom step of rostrum.*) He was coughing to disguise his giggle, but that didn't deceive me for a moment.

LADY INDIA. Anyway, why should this young man, who has nothing to do with me, giggle because he's found out we're having an affair?

PATRICE. Never mind why; mistrust him. (LADY INDIA *laughs and crosses to* R. C., *below couch.*) To begin with, there's this fantastic likeness to his brother.

LADY INDIA. He can't help that.

PATRICE. (*Moving* D. C.) My dear Dorothy. If he had any sense of propriety, he would never allow it to go on. He revels in it; he copies his brother's clothes.

LADY INDIA. No, dear, Frederic copies his.

PATRICE. Well, it's the same thing. (*He moves* U. L. *of couch.*) Now, I have eight brothers . . .

LADY INDIA. (*Moving above couch to* R. *of* PATRICE.) And they all look exactly like you?

PATRICE. Not at all.

LADY INDIA. I see. Then it doesn't help to convince me that this boy would say anything to Messerschmann.

PATRICE. *Say* anything, no; but little jokes and innuendoes when we're all in the drawing-room, yes. A mysterious chuckle in the middle of a meal, or a giggle like the one you thought was choking him with cigar-smoke; yes, most certainly.

LADY INDIA. Little jokes and chuckles will pass right over Messerschmann's head. (*Crosses, moves on to rostrum, stands on top step.*) He suffers from terribly poor reception.

PATRICE. (*Crossing to* L. *of* LADY INDIA, *standing beside her on ros-*

rum.) It's we who would have a poor reception if once he knew. Don't forget, you're his mistress and I'm his private secretary. We're both completely dependent on your magnate.

LADY INDIA. (*Reproachfully.*) Dearest heart, you use the most curious words.

PATRICE. Magnate?

LADY INDIA. No.

PATRICE. Private secretary?

LADY INDIA. No. (*Leans against him.*) Patrice, darling, I know I give him the pleasure of paying my bills, and every night I let him *trail* along to my room to kiss my hand, but that means nothing, (*Puts both her arms around his neck.*) and you mean everything.

PATRICE. (*Disengaging himself, desperately.*) Dorothy! Do be careful. We're in the winter-garden ——

LADY INDIA. On a lovely spring morning.

PATRICE. The season is immaterial. All this glass. Everyone can see us. (*He comes* D. *steps, moves* D. L.) We're completely exposed.

LADY INDIA. Danger! Oh, that's wonderful; I love it; I like being mad more than anything. Did I ever tell you about the evening in Monte Carlo when I went to a little dockside café, absolutely naked—(PATRICE *moans, looks anxiously around.*)—except for a cloak and my diamonds? Quite alone, too, amongst all those drunken brutes.

PATRICE. At Monte Carlo?

LADY INDIA. (*Moving to* R. *of* PATRICE.) A little café where the croupiers used to sip a secret *bock* between sessions. I just smiled to see how their hands shook when they raised their glasses. (*Pauses.*) So let him come, let him catch us, let him murder us. I shall drive him off with a lash of contempt—it will be magnificent. (*Turns, moves, stands on bottom step.*)

PATRICE. (*Moving in to* L. *of her.*) Yes, Dorothy. (*He kisses her cheek.*)

LADY INDIA. Don't forget, Patrice, you belong to a most distinguished family, and I, after all, am Lady India. He should be very grateful that we take the trouble to infuriate him. (*Turns and moves up rostrum.*) Money isn't everything. (PATRICE *follows* LADY INDIA *and they exit* R. C. MME. DESMORTES, *seated in a wheel-chair, is pushed on* D. L. *by her companion,* CAPULET. HUGO

follows them on. CAPULET *stops at chair* D. C., *stands* L. *of it.*
HUGO *crosses above chair, stands* R. *of it.*)
MME. DESMORTES. Oodles, oodles, oodles? Whatever do you
mean, Hugo, that Mr. Messerschmann has oodles?
HUGO. He's as rich as Croesus.
MME. DESMORTES. Oh. I see—but what does he do with it all?
HUGO. Eats noodles.
MME. DESMORTES. You're being altogether too playful, Hugo.
HUGO. It's quite true. At every meal, without butter or salt, and
drinks water.
MME. DESMORTES. How very spectacular. And you tell me that
Dorothy India is ruining him?
HUGO. She would be, if anyone could be, but there's too much of
it even for her.
MME. DESMORTES. (*Remembering* CAPULET *is present.*) You're a
scandalmonger, Hugo, and I won't listen to you. You forget I'm
your aunt, and India's aunt. I'm an elderly woman, and I never
listen to anyone. (*Turns to* CAPULET.) Capulet—(CAPULET *moves*
D. L. *of chair.*)—go and look for my handkerchief. (CAPULET
exits D. L. *She takes a handkerchief from basket on her lap.*)
Now, between ourselves, do you really imagine he's keeping her?
HUGO. (*Squatting* R. *of chair.*) Between ourselves, without a
shadow of doubt.
MME. DESMORTES. It's monstrous, Hugo; humiliating.
HUGO. Utterly monstrous, but, between ourselves, why humiliating?
MME. DESMORTES. She is a FitzHenry. And through me, a Desmortes. If only your Uncle Antony were alive it would kill him.
Hugo, people are so unkind; they will think I invited Dorothy and
this nabob at the same time on purpose. They'll say I'm a party
to it. So should I.
HUGO. Everyone knows you invited Mr. Messerschmann and his
daughter because Frederic asked you to. Frederic is going to
announce his engagement to Diana tomorrow.
MME. DESMORTES. Yes. There's another puppy-witted piece of
folly. Fancy becoming so infatuated with that girl he even has to
ask her to marry him! When he was little he always looked so
sad and resigned when he came to kiss me on Christmas morning.
I used to call him St. Pancras. And now the poor lamb's to be
sacrificed. Can you bear to think of him being delivered over,

11

gagged and bound, in his morning coat and gardenia, to this Diana Messerschmann and her millions?

HUGO. (*Rising, crossing* D. R.) No, Aunt.

MME. DESMORTES. No, I should think not. If it had been you, it would have been different. I love it when the lamb turns round and eats up the high priest. But with poor little Frederic it won't even be funny. (*Takes box of snuff from her basket, takes a pinch of snuff.*)

HUGO. If the marriage takes place, Aunt.

MME. DESMORTES. (*With a sigh.*) And who can prevent it now?

HUGO. (*Crossing, moving up on to rostrum.*) Who knows who? (*Leans on post* R. *of steps.* CAPULET *enters* D. L. *She carries a handkerchief.*)

CAPULET. (*Moving to* L. *of chair.*) Here is your handkerchief, madam.

MME. DESMORTES. (*Taking handkerchief.*) Thank you, my dear. Trundle me into the sun, if you will. (CAPULET *pushes chair* D. R. C. ROMAINVILLE, *followed by* MESSERSCHMANN, *enters* R. C.) Good morning, dear Romainville.

ROMAINVILLE. (*Moving* U. L. *of couch.*) My dear friend. (*Takes off his hat, bows, then eases to fountain.*)

MME. DESMORTES. Good morning, Mr. Messerschmann. Have you had a good night's rest?

MESSERSCHMANN. I never sleep, Madame. (*Takes off his hat, kisses her hand.*)

MME. DESMORTES. Neither do I. (CAPULET *pushes chair* D. R., *turns it to face* L., *then stands above it.* MESSERSCHMANN *stands* L. *of chair.*) We must make an appointment with one another some time, and gossip while the rest of them snore. We can say the most terrible things about them; it will help to kill time. He takes such a lot of killing, that animal, don't you think? (*Offers him pinch of snuff.* MESSERSCHMANN *shakes his head.*) I'm a wicked person, Mr. Messerschmann. Are you?

MESSERSCHMANN. I am told so, madame.

MME. DESMORTES. How nice. We can be wicked together. That will amuse me very much. (*To* CAPULET.) Push, dear, trundle me away. (MESSERSCHMANN *turns, crosses* D. L. CAPULET *draws chair a little up stage, then turns it toward exit* D. R.) I told you I wanted to be in the sun. (*She stops chair by means of the wheel rings, turns it.*) Oh, Mr. Messerschmann, my butler tells me you only eat noodles?

MESSERSCHMANN. That is so, without butter and without salt.

MME. DESMORTES. And I believe you're a great friend of my niece Dorothy?

MESSERSCHMANN. Yes, I have the pleasure of Lady India's friendship.

MME. DESMORTES. Insomnia, Dorothy, and nothing but noodles! What a *very* interesting life. (*Turns chair sharply, wheels herself off* D. R. CAPULET *follows her off.* MESSERSCHMANN *exits* D. L. ROMAINVILLE *crosses below* HUGO *toward door* D. L.)

HUGO. Her train gets in at twelve-thirty.

ROMAINVILLE. (*Stopping, turning.*) No.

HUGO. It certainly does.

ROMAINVILLE. (*Moving, standing on top step* L. *of* HUGO.) I'm convinced it's all a great mistake. It's making me ill with nerves. Are you sure you're not mad?

HUGO. (*Moving* D. *one step.*) Quite sure. How about you?

ROMAINVILLE. Not at all sure. Suppose I don't co-operate?

HUGO. (*Moving to couch and sitting.*) A scandal, Romainville.

ROMAINVILLE. (*Angrily.*) What scandal, for God's sake? (*Moves to* L. *of couch.*) My relationship with this girl is absolutely irreproachable.

HUGO. Suppose I say to my aunt, "Our dear Romainville, feeling the approach of springtime in the air, and in order to make his visit to you a cheerful one, has fetched his little friend over to stay at the inn at St. Fleur: he goes to see her secretly three times a week." What do you say then?

ROMAINVILLE. That it isn't true. That I'm only interested in this girl, as I'm interested in butterflies and old furniture. Is it my fault if I'm known as a patron of the arts? (*Sits on his shooting-stick.*)

HUGO. No.

ROMAINVILLE. The child needed a holiday before she goes back into the ballet. She was rather pale—do understand that, Hugo— she was extremely pale. Anybody would have done the same thing. It's entirely a question of common humanity. I said to her: "Come and spend a few days at Auvergne with your mother." Who, for God's sake, is going to make trouble because I give a holiday to a poor girl who needs one? Certainly not your good aunt, who

13

buttonholes me every year for her local charities. (*Swivels around on his stick, waves his butterfly net as though catching butterflies.*)

HUGO. To a poor girl who needs a holiday, no. But to your mistress, (*Snatches net from* ROMAINVILLE.) Romainville—well, you know my aunt.

ROMAINVILLE. For God's sake, she isn't my mistress. I assure you she isn't, not the least bit.

HUGO. Who's going to believe you?

ROMAINVILLE. Everybody, because it's true.

HUGO. That's no help. It doesn't seem likely.

ROMAINVILLE. So according to you the truth means nothing.

HUGO. Nothing, dear boy, if no one believes it. (*Sound of a dinner-gong is heard off* L. *He rises, crosses* D. L.) Let's go amiably in to lunch. They'll be here any minute now. I've warned Joshua and he'll let me know. I shall come out and have a word with them, and then, during coffee, Joshua can tell my aunt that your niece has arrived.

ROMAINVILLE. (*Rising, crossing to* R. *of* HUGO.) But suppose my real niece comes on the same train?

HUGO. That's all right. I sent her a telegram from you; you told her that my aunt's invitation had been cancelled for the time being.

ROMAINVILLE. It's a trap! And all because you found me drinking an innocent orangeade with this little girl, in a cake-shop at St. Fleur.

HUGO. Exactly.

ROMAINVILLE. You're the devil!

HUGO. Almost.

ROMAINVILLE. Would you just tell me what you're up to?

HUGO. (*Crossing to* C., *stalking imaginary butterflies.*) A huge and dark design. (*The sound of dinner gong is heard off* L. *He crosses above* ROMAINVILLE *to* L. *of him.*) There's the second gong. So in to luncheon, Romainville. You shall know everything before you're very much older. (*Drops net over* ROMAINVILLE'S *head, pulls him off* D. L. *Stage is empty for a moment, then* JOSHUA *enters* R. C., *moves below couch, and beckons off* R. ISABELLE *enters* D. R. *She carries a small suitcase which she places on ground* D. R.. *She is followed on by her* MOTHER, *who also carries suitcase, which she places alongside* ISABELLE'S.)

JOSHUA. If the ladies would be so good as to take a seat, I will go and inform Mr. Hugo of their arrival. (*He exits* D. L. MOTHER

14

moves slowly above couch, looks around. ISABELLE *eases* D. R. C.)

MOTHER. Isn't it luxurious, Isabelle? Such taste. Such grandeur. Now this is the kind of atmosphere where I really feel myself.

ISABELLE. Yes, Mother.

MOTHER. Some people, you know, can only breathe where there's beauty and luxury. Take luxury away from them, and they go quite limp. *(Goes up steps, stands on downstage end of rostrum.)*

ISABELLE. *(Sitting on couch, at* R. *end).* Yes, Mother.

MOTHER. Always remember, Isabelle, your grandfather was the biggest wall-paper dealer in the town. We've even had two servants at the same time, not counting the shop assistants, of course. When I was your age your grandmother would never have let me go out alone.

ISABELLE. No, Mother.

MOTHER. No. *(Moves* D. *steps.)* The maid always followed three steps behind me. Three steps. It was wonderful.

ISABELLE. Yes, Mother.

MOTHER. *(Moving to* L. *of* ISABELLE.) Did you see the butler?

ISABELLE. Yes, Mother.

MOTHER. That dignity, that sort of quilted voice, extremely polite, but also slightly scornful, such a perfect manner. *(Mimics him, delightedly.)* "If the ladies would be so good as to take a seat." To take a seat. You see how beautifully he chose his words. *(Sits on couch,* L. *of* ISABELLE.) You know, dear, in my dreams of you, there's always a butler like that in the background.

ISABELLE. Oh, Mother, you know it's not ——

MOTHER. Ah, yes, there is. It's been a dream of mine that you shall have everything I've missed. I don't say very much, I know, but there are times when I suffer. For instance, when I see your hands getting rough and red from washing-up.

ISABELLE. Now, please, Mother ——

MOTHER. I know it means nothing to you, because you haven't my sensitive nature. And I know I don't help you as much as I should. If only I were a little stronger; but even so I have to think of my art. I have to preserve my hands for my piano. And then I never knew what it was to want for anything when I was a girl, so different from you, my poor child, so I mustn't expect you to understand me. You roll up your sleeves, you sing something, and abracadabra, everything's done; you think no more about it.

ISABELLE. It's the best way, Mother.

MOTHER. (*Putting arm around* ISABELLE.) I admire you for it. (*Leans her head against* ISABELLE'S.) But with my upbringing, and all my dreams which came to nothing, (*Sighs.*) I could never do it. I still have my dreams, but now they're for you, Isabelle: a quite different future for you, a future of luxury and beauty, with a little corner somewhere for your mother. You're artistic, you're pretty, a little more commonplace than I was, perhaps— that's owing to your father—but interesting and attractive. You will certainly please someone, I'm sure you will. What do you suppose the young man wants you here for? (HUGO *enters* D. L., *moves* L. C. MOTHER *and* ISABELLE *rise.*)

HUGO. Thank you for being so punctual.

MOTHER. (*Moving to* R. *of* HUGO.) Not at all. Punctuality is the politeness of princes, I always think. And I'm sure you'll agree with me.

HUGO. Oh, yes, indeed. (*He kisses* MOTHER'S *hand.*) And this is Miss Isabelle? I wasn't mistaken.

MOTHER. She's a charming child.

HUGO. More than charming.

MOTHER. Mr. Romainville must have spoken about her to you.

HUGO. (*Gazing intently at* ISABELLE.) He has indeed.

MOTHER. He is one of our dear Parisian friends.

HUGO. (*Rather coldly.*) Yes, I know. (*Crosses below* MOTHER *to* L. *of* ISABELLE.) How do you feel about this adventure, Miss Isabelle? The most essential thing is for you to enjoy it.

MOTHER. She is thrilled about it.

ISABELLE. All Mr. Romainville said was that you had asked us up to your house this evening.

HUGO. Nothing else?

ISABELLE. No, nothing.

MOTHER. I expect our friend meant it all to be a surprise.

HUGO. And why should you think I would ask you to come here?

ISABELLE. I don't know. To dance, I expect. I am a dancer.

HUGO. Not only to dance.

MOTHER. Not only to dance? (*Moves above* HUGO, *stands between him and* ISABELLE.) Now you're beginning to make me really inquisitive. (HUGO *reaches across in front of* MOTHER, *takes* ISABELLE'S *hand, draws her to him.*)

HUGO. There's a Ball being held in this house tonight. I need you

16

here to be very beautiful, more beautiful, indeed, than anyone else.

ISABELLE. I?

HUGO. Yes. Are you afraid?

ISABELLE. A little. (*Withdraws her hand.*) I'm not very beautiful, and so I wonder ——

HUGO. I rang up Paris this morning. Roeseda Soeurs are sending some dresses to choose from, and their best fitters. (*Dances a few steps to* L. C.) At the first note of the violins, you will be ready.

ISABELLE. (*Moving to* R. *of* HUGO.) But what am I supposed to do?

HUGO. Only to go serenely through the night like a butterfly venturing on moonlight. With the first light of day we'll set you free. (*Breaks a little* U. L. C. *To* MOTHER.) The engagement will be paid for in the usual way, and the dress will be hers.

MOTHER. (*Moving to* R. *of* HUGO; *simpering.*) Oh, but we didn't think for one moment ——

HUGO. But I thought. Now I must go back to the dining-room or they'll begin to wonder where I am. (JOSHUA *enters* D. L.) I'm sorry I can't make it less of a mystery to you. (*He passes* JOSHUA *across to* R. *of himself.*) Here is Joshua to show you to your rooms. He will bring you your lunch. No one must know you're in the house. As soon as I can I shall come and tell you what I want you to do. (*He exits* D. L. JOSHUA *crosses to* R., *picks up suitcases.*)

JOSHUA. If the ladies will be so good as to follow me. (ISABELLE *faces* L., *gazes after* HUGO.)

MOTHER. Thank you very much. (*To* ISABELLE.) What a distinguished boy, such beautiful manners. Did you notice, dear, how he kissed my hand? Wake up, dear, are you dreaming?

ISABELLE. No, Mother. Is he the one they call Hugo? Is he the one who asked us here? (JOSHUA *sighs and puts down suitcases.*)

MOTHER. Well, of course. So handsome, don't you think? Now come along, we're keeping the butler waiting. (*She crosses below couch to* R. C., *turns.*) Where are you, my dear, in the moon?

ISABELLE. (*Gazing* L.; *dreamily.*) Yes, Mother. (JOSHUA *picks up suitcases, and* MOTHER *and* ISABELLE *exit with him* D. R. *as* ——)

THE CURTAIN FALLS

SCENE 2

SCENE: *The same. The same evening. Before the Ball.*
The decorations for the Ball are partly completed. One
end of a string of large Chinese lanterns has been fixed
high up above downstage end of conservatory. Opposite
end of string is looped about six feet above steps to
rostrum. From this end of the cord a red drape is hang-
ing so that lower edge just touches top step, thereby
screening anyone standing on downstage end of rostrum.
A pair of steps stand C. Couch has been removed and
replaced by a plain bentwood chair. A champagne box
stands on end at foot of rostrum steps.
When curtain rises, MME. DESMORTES is seated in her
wheel-chair L. C., midway between the pair of steps
and champagne box.

MME. DESMORTES. (*Calling.*) Capulet! Capulet. What on earth
can she be up to? Capulet. Really, how marooned one is away
from a bell-rope. I might be Robinson Crusoe, and without any
of his initiative. If only one's governess, when one was a girl, had
taught one something practical like running up a flag of distress
or firing a gun. (JOSHUA *enters* D. L. *Carries a tool-box, crosses
below* MME. DESMORTES *to* R. *of conservatory, wanders around
tree and finally puts box on floor* L. *of trellis.*) Thank Heaven,
I'm on some sort of navigation route. Joshua. Joshua. (JOSHUA
looks vaguely around, then moves below chair R. C., *stands* D. C.
of pair of steps.) Put in to land for a moment, my dear man, and
rescue me. I was washed up here fifteen minutes ago, and I
haven't seen a living creature since.
JOSHUA. Not one, madam?
MME. DESMORTES. Not one, and they say the world is overpopu-
lated. I sent Mademoiselle Capulet to fetch the list of guests out
of my bureau. I might have asked her to restock the lake with
carp, the time it's taking her. (CAPULET *enters* D. L. *She is dressed
for the evening and wears a feather boa. Carries a list of guests.*)
Oh, there you are at last, Capulet. (CAPULET *moves to* L. *of
wheel-chair.* JOSHUA *returns to his tool-box.*) You left me here
with a broken brake—look, and I've had nothing to do but to go
over all my shortcomings *twice.* (CAPULET *crosses* MME. DES-

MORTES *to* R. *of her.*) If you'd been away any longer I should have started to regret them. Where have you been?

CAPULET. You said the list was in the left-hand bottom drawer, madam, but it was the right-hand top drawer.

MME. DESMORTES. That's just another way of looking at it. (*Takes list from* CAPULET.) Now—well, get to work. (JOSHUA *crosses below* CAPULET, *stands* D. R. *of wheel-chair.*) I must try and remember who all these names belong to. It is so difficult. Nowadays no one has any proper sense of family; people have perfectly good names and then go and produce the most unpredictable faces to go with them. I don't know how they expect to be recognized— (JOSHUA *crosses below wheel-chair to* L. *of it. He and* CAPULET *go on to their knees,* R. *and* L. *of wheel-chair, face upstage and examine the underside of it.*)—and, worse still, it encourages all those terrible people who go to parties without being asked. I remember an evening at the Baroness Grave-Toureau's. (*Looks around.*) Where is everybody? Capulet, are you listening? (CAPULET *rises.*) I was saying, I remember an evening at the Baroness Grave-Toureau's when—well, mend me—mend me. (CAPULET *kneels.*) Joshua! (JOSHUA *rises.*) I remember an evening at the Baroness Grave Toureau's when there were so many uninvited guests, the Baroness imagined she must be at someone else's party, and spent most of the evening looking for her hostess to say good-bye. Now —— (CAPULET *rises.* JOSHUA *shakes wheel-chair violently, then spins it round to* C., *facing* L.) Must you do that? Oh! Deliverance! Now, Joshua, we don't want an unfortunate episode like that. (*She wheels herself in to* R. *of* JOSHUA.) Do you understand, Joshua, we don't want any mistakes.

JOSHUA. Certainly not, madam; though, as madam says, faces these days have taken a haphazard turn—most inconsiderate.

MME. DESMORTES. You will have to look into them very carefully, Joshua, and so shall I. If one stares fixedly at an interloper's frontal bone, fixedly, Joshua, for a count of nine, a look of guilt will steal over it at once. Remember that. (*Turns her chair, wheels herself* D. R. CAPULET *moves to chair, starts to push it.* MME. DESMORTES *waves her away.*) I intend to stare myself, with great penetration, whenever the occasion offers.

JOSHUA. I hope and trust, madam, that no such occasional offering will ensue. It would be a cloud on an otherwise evening of

19

nice and aristocratic joy, which none of us would like to have to denounce, madam.

MME. DESMORTES. (*Wheeling herself to* C.) You're crumbling into a benevolent old man, Joshua. Denouncing—that's delicious; and I depend on you to see that we have no trespassers. (*Spins her chair to face* CAPULET. CAPULET, *startled, breaks* R. C. JOSHUA *moves below door* D. L. *To* CAPULET.) Come with me now, and we'll make a last inspection of the battlefield. Well, wheel, Capulet, wheel, my dear.

CAPULET. I feel so excited, really I do, madam, like a little yeasty bun in a good oven. (*She turns chair, wheels it* D. L.)

MME. DESMORTES. Oh, Joshua, what does the Prince of Palauge look like? (JOSHUA *fingers his chin doubtfully.*) Ah, yes, I remember—like a rather half-hearted resolution. (*She wheels herself off* D. L., *followed by* CAPULET *and* JOSHUA. *A short pause, then* HUGO *and* ISABELLE *enter* R. C. HUGO *crosses to* L., *closes the jalousies.* ISABELLE *crosses to* L. C.)

HUGO. All right; now walk towards me. (ISABELLE *takes a step or two* L.) Turn. (ISABELLE *pirouettes.*) Walk away again. (ISABELLE *moves* C. *and turns.*) You're perfect. (*He moves in to* L. *of her.*) What on earth are you trembling for? (*Orchestra for the Ball is heard tuning up off* L.)

ISABELLE. Scared.

HUGO. Scared of what? Of going to a party?

ISABELLE. Yes, I suppose so. The violins tuning up, a house full of strange people all at this moment dressing for the great occasion; and scared of the mystery you're making of it.

HUGO. And scared of me?

ISABELLE. Very much.

HUGO. You think I'm going to drag you into some shameful scene or other. (*Crosses to* R. C.) Romainville has been maligning me.

ISABELLE. (*Moving* C.) He said ——

HUGO. And of course you believed him?

ISABELLE. (*Gently.*) No.

HUGO. You should have believed him. When you discover what I've planned for this evening, you'll think I'm even worse than Romainville imagines. But you don't have to be afraid of bad people; they're just poor complicated devils like everyone else. It's only the fools who are formidable. (ROMAINVILLE *enters* D. L.

Crosses below ISABELLE *to* R. *of* ROMAINVILLE.) And here he is. We were talking about you. How are you this evening?

ROMAINVILLE. Very poorly, very poorly indeed. I'd been looking forward to this party very much, but I feel now as though I were going to an execution. I can't see why you want to go on with it.

HUGO. (*Turning to* ISABELLE.) He's afraid you'll lose your head among the knives and forks, or use a dessert spoon on the *foiegras,* and they'll all leap to their feet and say: "This can't be his niece at all. She's an impostor!" (ROMAINVILLE *closes jalousies.*) Just walk away a little. (ISABELLE *moves* D. R.) Now turn. (ISABELLE *pirouettes. He moves to* R. *of* ROMAINVILLE.) Look at that, Romainville. There's a niece for you. Between ourselves, old man, what's your niece really like?

ROMAINVILLE. (*Stiffly.*) She's a rather plain girl. Her nose is perhaps not as small as others. But she has an extremely nice character.

HUGO. It's clearly high time you replaced her. (*Crosses to* ISABELLE, *takes her hand, draws her across himself to* C.) Look at this girl in a dress like the smoke of bonfires. (ISABELLE *curtsies.*) You'll never see a niece more transparent, less of this world, or so entirely fashioned for a singular night of dancing in the early summer. (*Sits on chair* R.C.)

ROMAINVILLE. (*Crossing above* ISABELLE *to* R. *of her, solemnly inspecting her.*) Hold yourself upright. When you're presented to people don't address them by their titles. (*Moves above* ISABELLE *to* L. *of her.*) Always wait for an older person to speak to you. (*Crosses below* ISABELLE *to* R. *of her.*)

HUGO. Dear man, you're wasting your breath. Isabelle was waiting for older people to speak to her in the womb. My aunt has an infallible instinct for quality, and she's given her a room looking out on to the garden. If she hadn't had the highest opinion of her, she would have put her facing the park.

ROMAINVILLE. Not at all; I'm facing the park.

HUGO. (*Laughing.*) So you see what I mean. (MOTHER *enters* R. C. HUGO *rises, moves to* R. *of her,* ROMAINVILLE *to* L. *of her.*)

MOTHER. May I come in? May I come in? I couldn't keep away for another minute; I simply had to come and see the dress.

HUGO. (*Vexed.*) I thought it was agreed you should stay in your room. We don't want people asking who you are.

MOTHER. I came on tiptoe the whole way; you would have thought I was a shadow. I'm dying of curiosity. (*Pushes* ROMAINVILLE *aside, crosses to* R. *of* ISABELLE, *looks at her.*) Oh, how charming. Oh, how wonderfully elegant. Hold yourself up straight, dear. What good taste. I'm quite sure Mr. Hugo chose it himself.

HUGO. (*Breaking* D. R.) Not at all. (*Looks at his watch.*) Your daughter chose it.

MOTHER. Then I'm sure you had something to do with it. (*Crosses below* ISABELLE *to* L. *of her.*) Or else the child guessed your taste and chose it to please you.

ISABELLE. Mother!

MOTHER. Turn round, dear. (ISABELLE *pirouettes.*) Once again. (ISABELLE *pirouettes.*) Hold yourself up. (*To* HUGO.) She's a constant surprise to me. Dressed, you would think she's *such* a skinnygalee; undressed, she's almost plump. Raspoutini, her ballet-master, said it's quite simply because she is well-built. As a matter of fact, and I don't say it just because I'm her mother, she has very good legs. (*To* ROMAINVILLE.) This dear gentleman can bear me out, can't you?

ROMAINVILLE. (*Moving to* R. *of* ISABELLE; *embarrassed.*) Hm! I still think she looks extremely pale. We should give her a tonic. That's it, a splendid tonic.

MOTHER. Pale! How can you say so? Look at her, she's as pink as a strawberry.

ROMAINVILLE. Hm! The country air has done some good already, you see. There's nothing like the country, nothing like it.

MOTHER. How can you say so? The country is death to her. And to me. We're just hot-house flowers, two Parisians, two artists. In the countryside we just wait to be eaten by sheep. (*Crosses below* ISABELLE *to* L. *of* ROMAINVILLE.) Only our dear friend insisted we should come.

ROMAINVILLE. Her health comes first, her health comes first. (*Turns, moves to* L. *of* HUGO.)

MOTHER. (*Moving to* L. *of* ROMAINVILLE.) Isn't he domineering? His friends must do what he says; he can't bear not to have them with him. When he knew he was coming here, he wouldn't rest until the child came, too.

ROMAINVILLE. She looked extremely pale. I said to myself ——

MOTHER. Yes, yes; and we forgive you because we know you do

22

it out of friendship, just as you did when you made her learn to swim.

ROMAINVILLE. (*Increasingly embarrassed.*) Everybody should learn to swim. (ISABELLE *eases* U. L. *of ladder.*)

MOTHER. He came to the baths himself to watch her, and one day he fell in without taking his clothes off.

ROMAINVILLE. (*Beside himself.*) Didn't I say so, doesn't that prove everybody should learn to swim? (*Hustles* MOTHER D. L. C.) We've chattered quite enough; Hugo must be wanting to give Isabelle her instructions. And I know you'd like to see the carriages arriving. You can come up to my room; it faces north, but you can see everyone who comes to the door.

MOTHER. Yes, that's it, we'll leave them together. Of course I'm burning with curiosity to know what the mystery's about, but Isabelle will tell me tomorrow. Come along, then. I shall hide away like a dilapidated old moth who's been told not to dance round the candles.

ROMAINVILLE. (*Hustling* MOTHER *to door* D. L.) That's right. Like a dilapidated old moth. Off we go. I can hear the first carriages arriving already. (*Exits* D. L.)

HUGO. (*Calling.*) And you shall have supper brought up to you.

MOTHER. (*Stopping, turning.*) Just a crust, (*Moves* C.) a crust and a glass of water for poor little Cinders. Enjoy yourself, you fortunate girl. I was twenty once; and not so long ago either. (ROMAINVILLE *re-enters, crosses to* MOTHER, *turns her, pushes her to door* D. L.) She looks charming, charming. (*She exits, pushed off by* ROMAINVILLE.)

HUGO. (*Crossing to box* L. C.) And she's blushing.

ISABELLE. (*Easing* D. C.) With embarrassment.

HUGO. Needlessly.

ISABELLE. It's easy enough to talk. My cheeks burn, my eyes are stinging; I've a lump in my throat and I should like to be dead.

HUGO. (*Sitting on box.*) She amuses me.

ISABELLE. She might amuse me, too, if only ——

HUGO. (*Taking cigar from his case, putting it in his holder.*) If you had ever listened to what they call a society woman trying to put up the bidding for her daughter, you wouldn't be indignant any more. Your mother's discretion itself. (*Lights cigar.*)

ISABELLE. I'm not plump, nor a skinnygalee; I've not got very good legs. (*Moves toward door* D. L.) I don't want to stay here.

HUGO. (*Stopping her* R. *of him with gesture.*) You can't go yet.

ISABELLE. I feel so ashamed.

HUGO. Why should you be? Because this party and the slight air of mystery has kindled your mother's imagination? Because she likes to think I'm in love with you and tries to throw you at my head? It's most natural. I'm rich, I belong to an old family, and ever since I was marriageable I've heard mothers hammering out that old tune. If you're ashamed because of me, forget your blushes. I've heard the tune so often, I'm deaf to it.

ISABELLE. But I can still hear it.

HUGO. Yes, I can see it must be unpleasant for you. I'm sorry. (*A pause.*)

ISABELLE. (*Suddenly.*) Have you considered Romainville?

HUGO. Oh, now, I never do that. Romainville is scrupulous and considerate, but not considerable. I met you with him in a cake-shop at St. Fleur, I thought you were charming, and it occurred to me you might be very useful this evening. That's all.

ISABELLE. But I think you should know ——

HUGO. I don't want to know anything else at all. (ISABELLE *crosses below* HUGO *to* L. *of him.*)

ISABELLE. (*Softly, flatly.*) I see. (JOSHUA *enters* U. L., *comes down rostrum, moves to pair of steps, climbs up it.*) I only wanted to— to tell you —— (*Turns her back to* HUGO.) Oh dear, I'm silly. I've been crying, and now I shall have to begin my face all over again. Will you excuse me for a little while?

HUGO. Of course. (ISABELLE *exits* D. L. *He calls.*) Joshua.

JOSHUA. Mr. Hugo? (*Comes* D. *steps, stands* R. *of* HUGO.)

HUGO. Does anyone suspect anything?

JOSHUA. No one, sir. The dress-shop people and the shoeshop person have went, sir, unobserved. So many outside individuals here tonight, in any case, making the preparations ——

HUGO. You'll keep your eye on the mother.

JOSHUA. As far as the human eye can be kept, sir. I beg your pardon, but she escaped my notice just now. What with all the preparations for the Ball, sir ——

HUGO. If only she'll content herself with trotting between here and her room, it may be all right. But she'll worry me considerably once the evening has really begun. (*Locks an imaginary door with key.*) Click, click.

24

JOSHUA. Very good, sir. But supposing the lady were to scream? We have to look all eventualities in the face, sir.

HUGO. Tell her I told you to shut her in, and promise her two hundred francs extra.

JOSHUA. Certainly, sir. (*Turns, crosses above pair of steps to R. of it, then stops and turns.*) Excuse me, sir, but—you think that will be sufficient to—to quench this particular individual, sir?

HUGO. Quite sufficient.

JOSHUA. Very good, sir. (*Moves U. through conservatory, exits U. R. As he does so* ISABELLE *enters D. L.*)

HUGO. Everything all right again?

ISABELLE. (*Standing in doorway.*) Yes; no signs of tears now.

HUGO. It's very useful to be able to disappear, and come back with new eyes and a fresh smile, ready to pick up the conversation where you left off. The poor naked face of the male has to fight for a façade as best it can. (*Looks at his watch.*) It's almost ten o'clock; your dress makes you look like Helen of Troy: (*Rises, moves to R. of her, takes her R. hand, passes her across to C.*) the first carriages are grinding the gravel in the drive: the fiddlers are rubbing rosin on their bows: and it's time I explained things to you.

ISABELLE. High time. (HUGO *leads* ISABELLE *to chair R. C., sits her on it.*)

HUGO. I had to get to know you a little first. If you had been a fool I should have thought up a story for you, something picturesque and sentimental, a snip for a housewife's magazine. I'd begun to think of something like that when I asked you to come here. Something conventional; that's always the easiest. (*Leans against R. side of ladder.*) But, once in a very great while, something conventional is too threadbare for the circumstances, and a man's left standing stupidly with his intelligence on his arm, like a rolled umbrella he hadn't expected to use. So much the worse for me. Now I shall have to talk without preparation.

ISABELLE. I'm so sorry.

HUGO. Not at all. (*Moves to L. of her.*) It's my fault for being such a poor judge of character. I ought to have been able to tell at a glance. You're not a fool, you have simplicity; you're not romantic, you're tender; you're not hard, you're exacting. Each one is almost like the other, but in fact they're opposites. This will teach me to look carelessly at girls in cake-shops. I'd thought of

25

everything except one. (*Kneels* L. *of her.*) I didn't expect you to look at me with such penetrating eyes.

ISABELLE. If it upsets you I can shut them.

HUGO. Not at all; your penetration will save time. I can cut the preamble and get to the point. Now, listen. I have a brother who is addled with love for a rich, young, beautiful girl. This party is in her honor.

ISABELLE. And she doesn't love him?

HUGO. She's engaged to him, which means that she gives him her lips two or three times a day, and lets him have contact occasionally with her pretty, lukewarm hand, while she turns her mind to something else. She makes all the loving gestures expected of her, she even tells him she loves him, but she doesn't.

ISABELLE. Does she love someone else?

HUGO. I should say she's quite incapable of loving anybody. But as she's a little multi-millionairess, and badly spoilt, blown sky-high by every breeze of a whim, she's made herself believe—yes, that she loves someone else.

ISABELLE. And that person is ——

HUGO. (*Rising.*) As you've so quickly guessed, myself. (*Moves* D. C.) You'll tell me she must be extremely stupid, because my brother is at least a thousand times nicer than I am.

ISABELLE. What does he look like?

HUGO. You see, that's the devil of preparing speeches in advance. I've forgotten to tell you the most important thing. We're twins.

ISABELLE. You look like each other?

HUGO. Physically, we're so alike it's neither permissible nor proper. (*Moves to pair of steps, leans against it.*) But morally—morally, we're as different as day and night. My brother is good, sensible, kind, and intelligent; and I'm the reverse. But nevertheless she loves me and not him.

ISABELLE. (*Rising.*) And you?

HUGO. I?

ISABELLE. (*Moving to* R. *of* HUGO.) You love her, perhaps?

HUGO. I love nobody. That's why I can organize this evening's little comedy with complete serenity. (*Moves to* L. *of pair of steps, goes up two or three steps.*) I'm acting providence tonight. I deflect the influence of the stars. The stars, twinkling up there, without an inkling of what's going to happen tonight. Now this is what I want you to do.

ISABELLE. (*Crossing* D. L. *of pair of steps.*) Tell me.

HUGO. To begin with, unquestioning obedience, and keep your eye on me all the time. I can only give you the broad outline; the details will have to be worked out as the evening goes on. Don't be afraid, you'll never be alone. I shall appear from behind a screen; I shall be behind the sofa where you go to sit with your partner, or under the tablecloth, or lurking in a shadow in the garden. I shall be everywhere, always watching you and whispering my orders to you. It's very simple. All you've got to do is to become the center of interest; the party must revolve round you and no one else.

ISABELLE. You're expecting too much of me. I can never do it.

HUGO. I can do it. Don't be afraid, be yourself. Say whatever you want to say. Laugh whenever you want to laugh. (*Comes down pair of steps, moves to* L. *of* ISABELLE.) If you suddenly feel like being alone, be alone. I shall expound you brilliantly; I shall make everything you say or do seem enchanting, extravagant and witty. I shall make them all think I'm in love with you.

ISABELLE. (*Happily.*) Will you?

HUGO. And you will make them all think you're in love with my brother.

ISABELLE. But if your brother is in love with this other girl, he won't even look at me.

HUGO. Being a fool, perhaps he won't. But even if he never takes his eyes off Diana, her eyes will tell him that you're the beauty of the evening. (*Crosses below* ISABELLE *to* R.) She will be *so* jealous.

ISABELLE. (*Moving to* L. *of chair.*) It will make your brother love her more than ever.

HUGO. You think so? What a pretty idea of love you have in the theater. No, put your mind at rest; I have everything nicely worked out. My brother is going to love you. It's all a question of waking him up. Diana isn't remotely the sort of girl he would want to love. (*Crosses below* ISABELLE *to* L. C.) He's suffering in his sleep, walking along a parapet of infatuation, and we're going to waken him.

ISABELLE. (*Moving to* R. *of* HUGO.) Suppose he should die of it?

HUGO. Whoever died of love? (ROMAINVILLE *enters excitedly* U. L., *comes* D. *through conservatory, and stands between* ISABELLE *and* HUGO.)

27

ROMAINVILLE. (*As he enters.*) Hugo. Hugo. Oh—there you are, there you are. I've been looking everywhere for you. Catastrophe!

HUGO. What do you mean—catastrophe?

ROMAINVILLE. My dear boy, the whole idea's exploded. Thank God!

HUGO. What are you talking about?

ROMAINVILLE. (*To* ISABELLE.) I was shepherding your mother back to her room, relying on the corridors being fairly dark, and we turned a corner slap into the Capulet.

ISABELLE. Capulet?

ROMAINVILLE. His aunt's companion.

HUGO. Well, you could pass that off all right.

ROMAINVILLE. I passed right on. But what did they do? They threw themselves like a pair of idiots into each other's arms, and burst into tears. It seems that they took piano lessons together at the *Mauberge Conservatoire*. (HUGO *crosses below* ROMAINVILLE *and* ISABELLE *to* R.) They've been thinking each other dead for twenty years. (*Crosses below* ISABELLE *to* L. *of* HUGO.) But, astonishing as it may be, they're alive. I was completely helpless. They're there still, looped around each other's necks, telling their life stories. Thank God they're both talking at once, and neither knows what the other is talking about. Whatever happens, there's only one thing for it: flight. (*Turns to* ISABELLE, *hustles her* D. L.) Go up and change. I shall say you've been taken ill, you've had a telegram, your grandmother's had a stroke; I'll say something or other. I've got an imagination, too. There's not a minute to lose. (*Moves above* ISABELLE, *stands above door* D. L.) Go up and change.

HUGO. (*Crossing to* ISABELLE.) Stay down here. (*Takes her hand, swings her across to* R.) I forbid you to go. (MOTHER *enters* D. L.)

MOTHER. (*Crossing toward* ISABELLE.) Coo-ee! (HUGO *stands* C., *bars* MOTHER *from* ISABELLE.) Have you heard my little piece of excitement?

HUGO. Yes. What have you been saying to her?

MOTHER. Oh, my dears, what bliss there can be in a friendship. (*Dodges quickly above* HUGO *to* L. *of* ISABELLE.) You've often heard me speak of Geraldine Capulet, haven't you, Isabelle? I thought she was dead, but she's alive, the dear sweet soul. What have I been saying to her? Why, everything, everything, you know: my unhappy marriage, the end of my artistic career, in

28

fact all my disappointments. You don't know what Geraldine has been to me. Both of us with golden hair; we were always taken for sisters.

HUGO. How did you explain your being in this house?

MOTHER. Quite simply. Did you think I should be taken off my guard? I told her I was one of the orchestra.

HUGO. } (*Together.*) {Ouf! (HUGO *breaks* U. R. C. *above*
ROMAINVILLE. } {*chair.* ROMAINVILLE *sits on box* L. C.)

MOTHER. But she didn't believe me. (*Crosses to* R. *of* ROMAINVILLE.) It wasn't a fortunate choice. It appears they are all negroes. (ISABELLE *crosses* L. *of pair of steps.*) So then do you know what I did? I have complete confidence in Geraldine. I made her swear on our long friendship that she wouldn't say a word to anybody, and I told her everything.

HUGO. } (*Together, in panic.*) Everything? (HUGO *breaks*
ROMAINVILLE. } D. R. ROMAINVILLE *rises, moves* D. L., *closes jalousies.*)

MOTHER. Everything.

HUGO. (*Crossing to* C.) What do you mean everything? (ROMAINVILLE *eases above box* L. C.) You know nothing about it.

MOTHER. No, but you know I'm quick with my little romances; like a big child, really; I'm incorrigible. I embroidered something to suit the case, a little figment.

ROMAINVILLE. A little figment?

HUGO. What little figment? (*Crosses below* ISABELLE *to* R. *of* MOTHER. ISABELLE *eases* D. R. *of pair of steps.*)

MOTHER. A little rosy-colored figment. Oh, dear, I believe you're going to scold me.

HUGO. Let's get to the point: what exactly have you said?

MOTHER. Nothing: just foolishness, words, day-dreams. I said you were in love with my little girl, and you wanted to bring her here without a lot of to-do—(HUGO *crosses to* R. *of chair* R. C.)— so you were pretending she was Mr. Romainville's niece.

ISABELLE. (*Easing* C., *distressed.*) How could you say such a thing?

ROMAINVILLE. Good heavens! My dear Hugo, by now your aunt knows the whole thing. I don't know what you're going to do, but I'm leaving. (*Moves to door* D. L.) It's a great pity, I shall never be able to come here again. Our whole life gets altered by accidents. (*Crosses, to* L. *of* ISABELLE.) Go upstairs and change, for goodness' sake.

HUGO. (*Crossing to door* D. L.) I must find Capulet. I must tell her to keep her mouth shut. (MME. DESMORTES, *pushed by* CAPULET, *enters* D. L. ROMAINVILLE *hurriedly pushes* MOTHER *into hiding behind red drape at top of rostrum steps, then stands* L. *of ladder.* ISABELLE *breaks* D. R. *Sound of waltz music is heard off* L. *During ensuing speeches a* FOOTMAN *enters* D. L., *picks up box* L. C., *exits with it* D. R. *A second* FOOTMAN *enters* D. R., *removes pair of steps, chair and tool-box, taking them off* D. R.)

MME. DESMORTES. Where are you off to, Hugo dear?

HUGO. (*Easing* D. L. C.) Nowhere in particular.

MME. DESMORTES. Then stop behaving like a cul-de-sac. (*Waves* HUGO *aside.* HUGO *eases a few steps* U. C. CAPULET *pushes chair to* R. C. ISABELLE *curtsies, stands* D. R. *of* MME. DESMORTES.) I've come to see my young guest. Why hide her away in this hole and corner? (*Pauses, surveys* ISABELLE. *To* ROMAINVILLE.) I congratulate you, my dear friend. (ROMAINVILLE *moves to* L. *of* MME. DESMORTES. HUGO *eases* D. L.)

ROMAINVILLE. (*Startled, suspiciously.*) Congratulate me? Why congratulate me?

MME. DESMORTES. She's very charming.

ROMAINVILLE. No!

MME. DESMORTES. No?

ROMAINVILLE. Yes!

MME. DESMORTES. Is she well and happy?

ROMAINVILLE. Not—not just now. Rather faint.

MME. DESMORTES. What nonsense are you talking? Her cheeks are like roses. One dance will put her on top of the world.

ROMAINVILLE. (*Beside himself.*) She's afraid of getting a telegram.

MME. DESMORTES. That's a curious anxiety. What a very pretty dress you're wearing! Is that your present to her, you generous man?

ROMAINVILLE. (*Easing* L. C.) Certainly not.

MME. DESMORTES. I hope you like your room, my dear. Tomorrow morning you'll get the very first of the sunshine. Do you mean to enjoy yourself this evening?

ISABELLE. Oh, yes!

MME. DESMORTES. (*Turning her chair to face* ROMAINVILLE.) Who was it told me it was your first Ball?

30

ROMAINVILLE. It wasn't I.

MME. DESMORTES. Was it you, Hugo? No, of course not; you don't know her. I hope someone has introduced you?

HUGO. Yes, Aunt, someone has introduced us.

MME. DESMORTES. She's entrancing, isn't she?

HUGO. Entrancing.

MME. DESMORTES. Why don't you ask her to dance? They're playing the first waltz.

HUGO. (*Crossing to* L. C.) I was about to. (*Holds out hand to* ISABELLE.) Will you give me the pleasure of this waltz, mademoiselle? (ISABELLE *crosses to* HUGO, *takes his hand, curtsies, then exits with him* D. L. *As he exits. To* ROMAINVILLE.) She's bluffing. She doesn't know a thing. (MME. DESMORTES *turns her chair to face front.*)

ROMAINVILLE. She knows everything. (MOTHER *comes out of hiding, unseen my* MME. DESMORTES. ROMAINVILLE *moves quickly to* MOTHER, *hustles her behind tree.*)

MME. DESMORTES. She is exquisite, she is pretty, and she's well-bred. How is it, Romainville, you've never talked about her to me?

ROMAINVILLE. (*Moving to* R. *of* MME. DESMORTES; *unhappily.*) I don't know. I can't explain it at all—not even—not even to myself. (MOTHER *comes from behind tree, moves above trellis, peeps out* L. *of it.* CAPULET *removes her boa, drops it on floor behind her.*)

MME. DESMORTES. Let me think, now: on her mother's side, if my memory serves, she is a Dandinet-Dandaine.

ROMAINVILLE. Yes, but ——

MME. DESMORTES. Then she's connected with the Rochemarsouins?

ROMAINVILLE. Perhaps, perhaps, but ——

MME. DESMORTES. If she's connected with the Rochemarsouins, she must also be a Cazaubon.

ROMAINVILLE. Yes, I suppose she must, but ——

MME. DESMORTES. My poor Antony was a Cazaubon through the Marsusses and the Villevilles, so he would have been as it were a slight relation—(MOTHER *comes out of hiding, stands* R. *of trellis.* ROMAINVILLE *peers anxiously over his* R. *shoulder*)—of hers if he had lived.

ROMAINVILLE. As it were—but as it is, he is dead.

MME. DESMORTES. But I'm still alive, Romainville, and I like to be quite clear about relationships. It's very important I should see

exactly how this girl fits in. (*Signs to* CAPULET *to push her* D. L.)
Now, you were saying her mother, who was a Fripont-Minet,
is dead.

ROMAINVILLE. (*Following chair.*) Dead.

MME. DESMORTES. Her mother's cousin, then, one of the Laboulasses ——

ROMAINVILLE. (*Interrupting.*) Also dead.

MME. DESMORTES. The one I went to school with? I don't mean
the younger one.

ROMAINVILLE. Dead, dead.

MME. DESMORTES. What, both of them? (*Stops chair in doorway*
D. L., *speaks over her shoulder.*)

ROMAINVILLE. Both of them.

MME. DESMORTES. And on her father's side: the Dupont-Pitard
family?

ROMAINVILLE. All dead.

MME. DESMORTES. Poor little thing! Why, she's living in a morgue.

ROMAINVILLE. A charnel house. (CAPULET *wheels* MME. DES.-
MORTES *off* D. L. ROMAINVILLE *follows them off. Music stops.*
MOTHER *eases* C., *looks off* L., *then turns and tiptoes* D. R.
CAPULET *re-enters* D. L., *runs to* MOTHER, *kisses her. Music of
waltz is heard off* L.)

CAPULET. I told them I had lost my boa. (*Moves to her boa, picks
it up, puts it on.*)

MOTHER. (*Moving to* R. *of* CAPULET.) To see you! To think that
I really see you. It's like a dream.

CAPULET. It is, isn't it, it really is. The whole thing, the whole
thing's such a romance, it really is. (*Moves to door* D. L.)

MOTHER. (*Following* CAPULET.) He worships her; you could see
it in every look he gave.

CAPULET. He's absurdly rich. It really is a romance.

MOTHER. And handsome as a lion. (*Takes* CAPULET *by the hand,
leads her* C.) You must help me, my dear, or my little girl will
die of it.

CAPULET. I'll do anything and everything. (*Puts her* R. *arm
around* MOTHER.) The whole thing's such a romance, it really is.
(*Puts cheek against* MOTHER'S.) Ah, dear! Our little wild whirling
days at Mauberge, can you remember them? The cake shop
Marius Laubonne.

MOTHER. And the ice creams at Pinteau's.

32

CAPULET. And the first duet we played together, at the Charity Concert for the Mauberge Widows' Fund. (*Listens to music for a few moments.*) That waltz.

MOTHER. That's the very waltz. (*Starts to sing the music.*) La, si, do, re, do, la, sol, la, sol, fa, mi, re, do. (MOTHER *and* CAPULET *stand for a moment rocking to and fro with their heads together, then* CAPULET *kisses* MOTHER, *breaks from her, backs to door* D. L. *and exits furtively, blowing kisses to* MOTHER *with her boa.* MOTHER, *eyes half closed, starts to waltz by herself.* JOSHUA *enters* U. L., *comes down steps and moves toward* MOTHER, *as though stalking a butterfly.* MOTHER, *without seeing him, waltzes across and exits* R. C. JOSHUA *follows her off.*)

CURTAIN

ACT II

SCENE: *The same. The same evening. The Ball. The decorations for the Ball are now complete. The line of Chinese lanterns and drapes is now fully suspended in festoons across front of conservatory. A small flowerbed has been laid against* L. *side of trellis* R. C. *and two small plush-and-gold chairs stand side by side below it, facing* D. L.
Before curtain rises music of a gay two-step is heard off L. *and continues softly as action starts. When curtain rises, stage is empty. After a few moments,* MME. DESMORTES *is pushed on* D. L. *by* CAPULET. *She pushes chair* D. R. C., *turns it to face front, then stands* R. *of it, fans herself.*

CAPULET. (*After a pause.*) Well, the Ball has really got going now, hasn't it, madam?

MME. DESMORTES. (*Peevishly.*) It can get going and go, for all I care. It bores me until I don't know whether to yawn or yelp. I was never fond of dancing, and since I've been screwed to this chair, it looks more than ever like the hopping of kangaroos. You've never liked it either, have you? (CAPULET *stops fanning and moves above chair to* L. *of it.*)

CAPULET. (*Simpering.*) I was a girl of twenty, you know, once upon a time.

MME. DESMORTES. (*Turning her chair to look at* CAPULET.) When, for goodness' sake? You've never looked any different to me.

CAPULET. Oh, yes, I was, madam. I was young when I was with the Baron and Baroness, before I came here.

MME. DESMORTES. Ah, well, you may have thought so. (*Signs to* CAPULET *to push chair a little up* R. C.) You're a nice girl, Capulet, but—you know this as well as I do—you're plain. No one who is plain can ever have been twenty.

CAPULET. (*Easing chair a little* U. R. C.) But a heart beats in my breast all the same, madam. (*Stands* L. *of chair.*)

MME. DESMORTES. My good soul, a heart with no face is more

34

bother than everything else put together. Let's talk no more about it. You've been quite happy, Capulet, without a face; you've been respected, and you've been appreciated. What could be nicer than that?

CAPULET. (*Moving up steps on to rostrum.*) On evenings like this, when there's music and the young people dancing under the chandeliers, I feel something indescribable in the air.

MME. DESMORTES. Then don't attempt to describe it. It's much too late. You really have nothing to grumble about. And there's always the life to come. A dull life in this world is a splendid recommendation for the next.

CAPULET. Oh, madam!

MME. DESMORTES. You will be hobnobbing with the Blessed while I'm roasting over a slow fire for two or three thousand years. Well, perhaps it won't seem so long.

CAPULET. (*Moving to* L. *of chair.*) God's mercy is infinite, madam.

MME. DESMORTES. Certainly; but He must abide by what He says, you know, otherwise the Just like you, who've staked everything on it, are going to feel very badly let down. Suppose a rumor started circulating among the Sheep that the Goats were going to be pardoned as well? They would use such bad language that hey'd get themselves damned on the spot. Don't you think it would be rather comic?

CAPULET. Oh, you can't really think that, madam.

MME. DESMORTES. Why not? I can think anything I like, it's all I have left to do. Push me nearer the doors where I can see the frisking of little fools. (CAPULET *wheels chair* L., *leaves it facing door* D. L. *She takes a pair of opera glasses from her basket and looks through them off* L.) Isn't that Romainville's niece dancing with my nephew?

CAPULET. (*Looking off* L.) Yes, madam.

MME. DESMORTES. She has a very unusual grace; the only woman who is being herself. Why didn't Romainville bring her here before?

CAPULET. She's so graceful, really she is, isn't she? She has such— what shall I say ——?

MME. DESMORTES. Whatever you care to, dear; I'm not listening. (*Turns chair to face* CAPULET.) Do you know what I think? I think you and I need amusing this evening Now, what can we think of to liven ourselves up?

CAPULET. (*Crossing to* R. C.) A cotillion?

MME. DESMORTES. A cotillion. That is so like you. You couldn't have suggested anything sillier. Except the ball itself. (*Turns chair, looks off* L.) Look at them twirling and twiddling. They think they're enjoying themselves, but all they're doing is twizzling their vain little heads. (CAPULET *crosses, stands above the chair. She turns her chair and moves* D. L. C.) The world isn't amusing any more; it's time I left it. The fabulous evenings I've known in my time! In Eighteen ninety-two, Capulet—(CAPULET *moves* D. L. *of chair.*)—at Biarritz, the Duke of Medino-Solar was out-of-this-world in love with the Countess Funela. (*Music stops.*) You won't guess what he did. They were giving a public assembly—a ridotto, it used to be called—and everyone had to be dressed in yellow. Well, the Duke came in green. It was the color of his mistress's eyes, but of course nobody was to know that. The rules of a ridotto were always very strict and they refused to let him in. The Duke was a Spaniard of the hottest and bluest blood. Without any attempt to explain, he killed the footman. Of course the Ball went on. Their Highnesses the Infantas were there, so it was decided that anonymity should still be respected. The police were brought in, wearing yellow dominoes, and if you happened to dance with them you could see their beady eyes and really horrible moustaches under their masks. But, as they could only dance with the ladies, they weren't able to spot the Duke. The next day he crossed the frontier and a bull killed him in Madrid. (*Takes a pinch of snuff.*) That's what living used to be. (*Takes* CAPULET'S *fan and fans herself.*)

CAPULET. Yes, of course, but one doesn't know, really one doesn't; (*Eases above chair.*) romantic things may be going on here, at this very moment.

MME. DESMORTES. At this Ball? Dear Capulet, you should go and lie down. (*Signs to* CAPULET *to push her* D. R.)

CAPULET. (*Pushing chair* D. R.) Perhaps so, but perhaps not so. (*Turns chair to face* L.) Suppose there was a young, rich, handsome man, spellbound with love, who had smuggled his loved one into the Ball . . . but I've said too much. I promised I wouldn't breathe a word.

MME. DESMORTES. Why should I suppose there was any such person?

CAPULET. (*Easing above chair to* R. C.) And, as well as the young man, an old friend, a dear, dear friend given up for dead, suddenly coming back like the bluebells in May. (MME. DESMORTES *signs to* CAPULET *to sit. She sits in downstage chair.*) It's really wonderful, it really is, suddenly to take part in a fairy story.

MME. DESMORTES. Bluebells? Fairy story? Capulet, I don't know what you're talking about.

CAPULET. To think the work is still so colorful, madam, it really is. Love can still be stronger than social barriers, careless of scandal, as pure as death. There can still be the desperate plot, the impersonation, madam. And the poor apprehensive mother, hiding herself away and watching her child's triumph without ever—ever —— (*Rises, goes to* R. *of wheel-chair, dabs her eyes.*) Oh, I really can't stop the tears, madam, I can't really: I'm so sorry.

MME. DESMORTES. Suppose you explain yourself, Capulet, instead of watering my hair. What apprehensive mother, what impersonation?

CAPULET. Oh, I've said too much. I promised I wouldn't breathe a word.

MME. DESMORTES. Promised whom, for Heaven's sake?

CAPULET. It's a secret, madam; the diamond at the bottom of a mine. (*Music of a waltz commences off* L.) She loves him, he worships her, she is poor, he brings her here disguised. It's really like a fairy story, really it is, isn't it?

MME. DESMORTES. She? He? Who are these people?

CAPULET. (*Rocking wheel chair.*) Everyone is either whispering her name or asking who she is. She moves among them like a queen. Her evening of triumph. (*Gives chair a sharp push* C.) And her mother played the treble and I played the bass, all those years ago ——

MME. DESMORTES. (*Stopping chair abruptly.*) Capulet!

CAPULET. (*Backing away* R. C.) I'm so sorry; do forgive me; it's all too much.

MME. DESMORTES. (*Turning chair to face* CAPULET.) Capulet, you've been my companion for twenty years, and though you've never said anything that amused me I've always been able to understand you. At last you interest me, and I can't understand a word. Either you explain, or you leave my service.

37

CAPULET. I promised not to breathe a word. I'd rather die in poverty; I'd rather you killed me.

MME. DESMORTES. I wouldn't dream of it. I'm used to being obeyed without having to kill people. And you know I always give you my old clothes. (*Wheels herself to* L. *of* CAPULET.) Don't I deserve a little consideration?

CAPULET. I know, I know that, madam. (*Crosses above chair to* L. C.) I'm being nearly torn apart by the two duties. (MME. DESMORTES *turns chair to face* CAPULET.) Oh, madam, we were such friends, we both played on the same piano. Such happy days. I thought she was dead, and I found her again. She told me she belonged to the orchestra, but they were all Negroes. I was astonished. Then she confided in me, and swore me to secrecy. All about the mad love of this young man for her daughter, and the stratagem of the good kind friend.

MME. DESMORTES. What good kind friend?

CAPULET. Monsieur Guy-Charles Romainville, such a good kind man.

MME. DESMORTES. What has he done?

CAPULET. His niece is not his niece. Love snaps its fingers. A young man who is very close to you. But I've said too much. I promised not to breathe a word.

MME. DESMORTES. Promised whom?

CAPULET. My dearest friend. (*Moves and leans against upstage jalousie of door* D. L.) I promised on the days of our duets. (MME. DESMORTES *wheels herself to* R. *of* CAPULET.) So better to die. (*Looks off* L.) Oh, madam, the violins. They're like strong wine to me.

MME. DESMORTES. So I've noticed, *mon amie.* Push me to my room where we shan't hear them, and tell me the rest of it. (*Music off* L. *ceases.*)

CAPULET. (*Kissing* MME. DESMORTES' *hand.*) You're so good, madam; there's nothing you can't do. (*Turns chair to face* R.) A word from you, and all the obstacles will evaporate.

MME. DESMORTES. Well, we shall see about that. Trundle me off and explain things without falling over yourself. You were saying that Romainville's niece ——

CAPULET. (*Pushing chair* D. R.) Is not his niece, madam. She's your nephew's loved one. He wanted her to be the belle of the Ball.

MME. DESMORTES.		My nephew? Which nephew?
CAPULET.	(*Together.*)	Frederic? Out with it,
		Capulet.

So he had a dress brought from Paris for her, and he begged her mother, my dear sweet friend —— No, madam. Mr. Hugo. But, oh dear, I'm sure I've said too much. I promised not to breathe a word. (*She wheels* MME. DESMORTES *off* D. R. *Music of a tango commences off* L. LADY INDIA *and* PATRICE *enter, dancing* D. L. *They dance a Mexican tango which continues simultaneously with following speeches. As they enter* PATRICE *has his back to line of dance. They pause below rostrum steps.*)

PATRICE. They've put me in a room looking out on the park, facing direct north—it's most unkind—and they've moved all my things in the middle of the afternoon, without telling me. They said they couldn't find me, but they're not going to make me believe that. (*They dance* D. R.) I never left the billiard-room. They couldn't find me because they didn't want to find me. (*They dance across to* L. *as* LADY INDIA *speaks and* PATRICE *replies.*)

LADY INDIA. Then who has got your room?

PATRICE. Romainville's niece. The girl with the lovely eyes. But that is only the excuse. The real reason is that he saw us together yesterday, and wants to have me further away from your room.

LADY INDIA. Nonsense! He would have to explain it all to my aunt. (*They hesitate,* D. L.) You mustn't be idiotic. And how do you know she has lovely eyes?

PATRICE. Who, dear heart?

LADY INDIA. This niece of Romainville's.

PATRICE. Have I said so?

LADY INDIA (*Backing to* L. *of chairs* U. R. C.) Now be careful, Patrice. (PATRICE *follows her.*) I don't like competitors. And if Messerschmann has seen us together and feels like braining you, I shall quite understand. Frankly, Patrice, I should be very disappointed if he didn't. (*She dips toward* PATRICE.) Don't you agree? (PATRICE *catches her and they dance three long dipping steps* D. R. *and turn.*)

PATRICE. Well, I suppose—I don't know—I suppose so. (*Both drop on to one knee and pose* D. R.)

LADY INDIA. I may deceive Messerschmann, but I like to think well of him. The man I love must be noble and courageous, and

39

the man I deceive must be noble and courageous, too. (*They rise.*) It gives life a kind of dignity which is most pleasing. (*Both dance three steps to* C., *swinging back to back.*) Surely, Patrice, you, so proud and susceptible, would be terribly upset if he didn't give a savage cry of uncontrollable jealousy?

PATRICE. I—well, Dorothy, I —— (*He dances solo* R. *with small crossover steps.*)

LADY INDIA. Exactly? Men of your calibre wouldn't want a woman who wasn't fiercely loved already. Creatures such as ourselves have no patience with the luke-warm. (PATRICE *returns to* C.) We blaze! Other people may be born to live, but we're on earth to blaze. (*Extends her arms and clasps her hands behind* PATRICE'S *neck.*)

PATRICE. Yes, Dorothy. (*They dance sideways* U. *and* D. C., *using a long crossover step with a kick.*)

LADY INDIA. And it's very nice of us to bother about him at all. Suppose he does ruin us? What fun it would be to be poor . . . as long as one was *excessively* poor. Anything in excess is most exhilarating. (*Back-bends over* PATRICE'S R. *arm.*)

PATRICE. Yes, Dorothy.

LADY INDIA. Our squalor would seem like a great dark poem, wouldn't it, Patrice?

PATRICE. Very dark. (LADY INDIA *breaks away to* L. *and they dance solo for a few lines of dialogue,* PATRICE *with his back to the audience at* C.)

LADY INDIA. How amusing it would be. I should wash the dishes, and clean the flues, whatever that may be, and bake and brew. How beautifully I should brew. I must ask Reseda Soeurs to make me some affecting little aprons. There's no one else, you know, who so well understands my style. (*Dances above* PATRICE *to* R. C. PATRICE *turns and faces her.*) What miracles she will do with a scrap of muslin and a ruche. And then I shall set to work with my tiny dustpan and my tiny broom. And you will work in a factory. (*Moves in to* R. *of* PATRICE.) You will come home in the evening, nearly dead with fatigue, and smelling dreadfully. It will be absolutely delicious. And I shall wash you down, my dear, from head to foot with a tiny sponge. It's beautiful to be poor, Patrice.

PATRICE. Beautiful? (MESSERSCHMANN *enters* U. R., *stands above tree, not daring to approach.*)

LADY INDIA. Let him come. (*They dance* D. R. *of chairs.*) What is he waiting for? His money is burning my fingers. I shall give it all back, immediately, (*Back-bends over* PATRICE'S R. *arm.*) everything except the pearls. (PATRICE *becomes aware of* MESSER-SCHMANN, *breaks from* LADY INDIA, *sits on downstage chair.*) PATRICE. (*Terrified.*) Do be careful—he's here. Do be careful. LADY INDIA. (*Standing above* PATRICE *with her back to* MESSER-SCHMANN.) Don't be such a coward, Patrice. PATRICE. I don't like you. I've never liked you. I'm never likely to like you. LADY INDIA. What? PATRICE. I'm only with you out of sheer necessity. It's quite obvious you bore me. Anyone can see that I'm yawning. (*He yawns.*) LADY INDIA. Patrice, don't dare to yawn. (*Takes his hand, crosses* D. R. *of him, draws him to his feet.*) Take my arm. (*They dance to* L. C. *with three long dipping steps.*) We'll go away, dancing as ostentatiously as possible. PATRICE. You're crazy. LADY INDIA. When the bull is drowsy, one stirs it up with a banderilla. (*They dance* D. R. *Loudly.*) Have you ever seen a bull-fight, dear friend? PATRICE. (*Loudly.*) Yes, dear friend, but I didn't like it. LADY INDIA. (*Sotto voce.*) Hold your head up. Don't look as though we've seen him. He needn't know yet we know he knows. (*They dance three long alternative crossover steps with a kick.*) PATRICE. Yes, but perhaps he doesn't know, Dorothy. Don't you think that by seeming to know we know he knows we run the risk of making him know? (*They exit, dancing* D. R. JOSHUA *enters* U. L., *moves on to rostrum. Music stops.* MESSERSCHMANN *moves* D. R. C., *looks after* LADY INDIA, *then turns, calls to* JOSHUA.) MESSERSCHMANN. Come here, my friend. JOSHUA. Sir? MESSERSCHMANN. The two people walking along the terrace there; they'd be making for the greenhouses, I suppose? JOSHUA. (*With a casual glance off* R.) Yes, sir. (*Pauses.*) Would you care to give me your order for supper, sir? MESSERSCHMANN. Noodles. JOSHUA. Without butter, sir? MESSERSCHMANN. And without salt.

41

JOSHUA. Very good, sir.

MESSERSCHMANN. (*After a pause.*) Tell me, my friend ——

JOSHUA. Sir?

MESSERSCHMANN. —If I go down those steps, I get to the greenhouses through the orchard, do I not?

JOSHUA. Yes, sir. (*Comes* D. *steps to* L. *of* MESSERSCHMANN.) But if you are hoping to catch up with the lady and gentleman, sir, I take the liberty to say that I've been watching the lady and gentleman, sir, while you were giving me your order, and they've come back into the house by the small door at the end of the terrace. The lady and gentleman have gone upstairs by the little staircase, sir.

MESSERSCHMANN. (*Crossing to* L.) I see.

JOSHUA. (*Moving in to* R. *of* MESSERSCHMANN.) No doubt the lady and gentleman wish to tidy their persons up, as it were, sir.

MESSERSCHMANN. (*Sighing.*) No doubt, yes. Thank you. (*Moves to door* D. L.)

JOSHUA. (*Bowing.*) Without butter.

MESSERSCHMANN. (*Sighing, somberly.*) And without salt. (*He exits* D. L. JOSHUA *exits* L. C. *Music of a waltz commences off* L. FREDERIC *enters* R. C., *crosses thoughtfully to exit* D. L. *He seems to be looking for something.* ISABELLE *enters* R. C., *moves to* R. *of chairs.* FREDERIC *exits* D. L. *and re-enters immediately, still searching* L. C. *Sees* ISABELLE, *moves* C. *They stand, looking at one another, a little uncomfortably, for a few moments.*)

ISABELLE. I hope you'll forgive me?

FREDERIC. For what, mademoiselle?

ISABELLE. I must seem to be following you. (*She takes step toward him.*) I happened to come in here and—and found you were here before me.

FREDERIC. Yes, of course.

ISABELLE. I'm enjoying—enjoying the evening very much.

FREDERIC. Yes, it's splendid. (*A pause. Making conversation.*) That's a very pretty dress you're wearing.

ISABELLE. Yes, it is pretty. (*Pauses. With a step forward, suddenly.*) Do you believe in them, I wonder?

FREDERIC. Believe in them?

ISABELLE. In ghosts.

FREDERIC. A little. Why?

ISABELLE. You look as though you might be your brother's ghost, made very sad by something.

FREDERIC. It's what I am.

ISABELLE. You're young, you're handsome, and you're rich. What can possibly have made you sad?

FREDERIC. Being handsome, as you call it, being young and rich, and nothing to be gained by it. (*Breaks* D. L. C.) Will you excuse me if I leave you now?

ISABELLE. Yes, certainly. (FREDERIC *exits* L. C. ISABELLE *watches him off, runs* D. L. C. HUGO *enters briskly* D. L., *moves to* L. *of* ISABELLE, *who backs* D. C.)

HUGO. That was perfect.

ISABELLE. I didn't know what to say. I feel very shy with him.

HUGO. Excellent!

ISABELLE. He'll wonder why I'm always at his elbow, and why I keep trying to speak to him.

HUGO. (*Taking* ISABELLE'S *hands.*) That's what I want.

ISABELLE. (*Breaking from him, sitting on upstage chair.*) I can't do it any more.

HUGO. (*Sternly.*) We're not yet past midnight, and you have a duty till dawn. Up you get. (*Moves to* L. *of her, claps his hands.*) You're a kindly creature, and this is a kindly action you're doing. I can promise you won't regret it. (ISABELLE *rises.*) That's right; look at him just as you're looking now. You're an astonishing actress. Where did you learn that look of deep regard?

ISABELLE. It's my own.

HUGO. Splendid! Turn it on Frederic from now till morning. (*Goes up on to steps, looks off* L.) He couldn't help being moved by it.

ISABELLE. (*Softly.*) It may be different when it turns on him.

HUGO. Well, something in the same line will do. Dear little brother; he's not used to being given pretty looks. (*Crosses below* ISABELLE *to* R. *of chairs.*) Look out, he's coming back. He wants to talk to you after all, you see. Now: compose yourself and use your imagination. I shall be listening. (*Exits* R. C. *As he does so, the* DOUBLE *quickly enters* R. C. *and hides in trellis.* ISABELLE *looks after* HUGO *for a moment.* DOUBLE *raps on trellis and indicates to her that she shall sit, then crouches above trellis. During this,* HUGO *passes quickly above backcloth and enters* L. C. *as* FREDERIC. ISABELLE *sits on upstage chair.*)

43

FREDERIC. (*Moving* D. C.) My brother was looking for you just now.

ISABELLE. Oh, was he?

FREDERIC. Usually, when my brother is looking for a girl, she knows it.

ISABELLE. Oh. I—I don't know.

FREDERIC. He's very good-looking; don't you think so?

ISABELLE. Yes—very.

FREDERIC. (*A step toward her.*) We're as alike as two blades of grass, but it's only men who get us confused. Women always know which is my brother. How do they do it?

ISABELLE. I don't know.

FREDERIC. It's because he doesn't look at them, maybe. (*Pauses.*) That's a very pretty dress you're wearing.

ISABELLE. Isn't it? He's not only good-looking.

FREDERIC. Who?

ISABELLE. Your brother.

FREDERIC. No. He's very intelligent; much more intelligent than I am. Very brave, too; completely fearless; always ready to shoot the rapids or put his hand in the fire. (*Music ceases.*) But there's one thing he couldn't ever do, not every day for any length of time. He couldn't be in love; and perhaps that's why they love him. He's very hard, but he's also very kind.

ISABELLE. He's very fond of you. He wouldn't like to see you hurt.

FREDERIC. It would irritate him. It's not so much that he's very fond of me. It annoys him to see me unhappy. He doesn't like people to be unhappy. Particularly unhappy in love. (*Crosses below* ISABELLE *to* R. *of chairs.*) Honestly, he's looking for you. If I come across him during my search shall I tell him where you are?

ISABELLE. Really, no. Thank you, but don't tell him.

FREDERIC. He's good company; much more so than I am.

ISABELLE. I like being with you. Please stay. (*Music of a waltz is heard off* L. FREDERIC *looks at* ISABELLE *in astonishment, then with a sigh sits on downstage chair.*)

FREDERIC. Oh! How sad it all is.

ISABELLE. How sad all what is?

FREDERIC. I'm sorry. What I'm going to say isn't very polite. Perhaps it's impolite, though I don't want to be impolite. But if the

44

girl I'm looking for so unsuccessfully had said what you have just said I might very well have died of happiness.

ISABELLE. (*Smiling sweetly at him.*) Then it's as well that it was I who said it. And it wasn't in the least impolite. I understand how you feel, only too well.

FREDERIC. (*Rising.*) Thank you for understanding, but forgive me all the same, and forgive me if I go now. (*Moves R. of the trellis.*)

ISABELLE. Of course. (*Music ceases. The DOUBLE and FREDERIC quickly change places. DOUBLE, with his back to audience, moves to exit R. C.*)

FREDERIC. (*Above trellis.*) Good-bye.

ISABELLE. Good-bye. (*DOUBLE exits. HUGO emerges L. of trellis and stands L. of ISABELLE, who rises, startled.*)

HUGO. (*Angrily.*) No, no, no! (*ISABELLE backs D. R.*) I didn't bring you here for that.

ISABELLE. What have I done?

HUGO. Sighing and hinting that you'd rather be with someone else. No more of that. You're paid to act a part, my dear, so act it. And without being ashamed of it. It's a serious job, and you should try to do it well. (*Moves to tree.*)

ISABELLE. (*Moving D. L. of HUGO; gently.*) Please don't go on.

HUGO. Why?

ISABELLE. If you went on talking to me in that voice, I should cry.

HUGO. Now that really would be a good idea. (*ISABELLE recoils D. L. C. He moves D. C.*) I wouldn't have suggested it myself. Manufactured tears always look a bit grotesque; but if you'll cry naturally, excellent! My dear little brother will founder at once.

ISABELLE. Why haven't you a heart?

HUGO. Because my brother has too much. We were born at the same time, and things were divided between us, this and that to me, a heart to him. (*Moves on to top step.*)

ISABELLE. (*Moving to foot of steps, L. of HUGO.*) But you must be able to see that I'm unhappy.

HUGO. Splendidly! You have a way of being unhappy that would fetch tears out of a rock. Have you a twin sister, by any chance, without a heart?

ISABELLE. I can't bear you.

HUGO. It's a very good thing you can't. Tell my brother so, and swim away with him in a flood of sympathy. (*Crosses to R. of chairs.*) That's just what I want.

ISABELLE. (*Crossing to* L. *of* HUGO.) You don't suppose I'm doing what I'm told this evening just for the sake of this dress and a fee for dancing?

HUGO. (*Moving to tree.*) My pretty one, I thought nothing so unpleasant.

ISABELLE. (*Easing* D. L. *of* HUGO.) I'm not interested in your brother, or in curing him, or in looking well-dressed, or in having everyone looking at me. Men have looked at me before even when I wasn't dressed well. (*Turns, moves* C.) Do you think that's amusing?

HUGO. (*Crossing above* ISABELLE *to* L. *of her.*) Don't fight back the tears any more, let yourself go. Cry, cry, cry, my dear. (ISABELLE *starts to weep.*) That's better. You see how easy it is.

ISABELLE. (*Crying.*) Now my eyes will be red. Isn't that rather clever of me?

HUGO. Superbly! (*Takes* ISABELLE *by hand, draws her up steps on to rostrum, kneels* R. *of her. Declaiming theatrically.*) Ah! Isabelle, dear Isabelle! I suffer too, I die as well!

ISABELLE. (*Drying her eyes.*) What are you doing?

HUGO. He's coming toward us. Stay just as you are. I want him to find me at your feet.

ISABELLE. Oh, no; this is dreadful.

HUGO. Yes, my darling. My heart is overflowing. I'm drowned in it. A heart in full flood. Is he coming toward us?

ISABELLE. Yes. Oh, please get up.

HUGO. (*Rising.*) Now's the time; all or nothing. Ah, well; I suppose I'd better kiss you. (*Takes her in his arms, kisses her.* ISABELLE *relaxes with a little cry.*)

ISABELLE. (*Suddenly.*) Why did you say "Ah, well"?

HUGO. (*Bowing, coldly.*) You must excuse me. (*Moves to door* D. L.) A kiss was necessary. (*Stands above downstage jalousie.*) Say to him, "Frederic, it's you I love." (*He exits and* DOUBLE *slips into place above downstage jalousie, with his back to audience. During following,* HUGO *passes quickly above backcloth to enter* U. R. *as* FREDERIC. *Music of a waltz commences off* L.)

ISABELLE. (*Moving to door* D. L. *and speaking off.*) No—please don't make me say I love him—I don't—I don't love him—I love —— (DOUBLE *points to steps.* ISABELLE *moves to steps and collapses on them, crying quietly to herself.* DOUBLE *exits.*

46

FREDERIC *enters* U. R., *crosses above conservatory and comes down rostrum to* L. *of* ISABELLE.)
FREDERIC. Are you crying?
ISABELLE. Yes.
FREDERIC. You ought to be happy; my brother kissed you. Usually when that happens, the girl is blushing and dancing like fire. But you're pale and you're crying.
ISABELLE. Yes.
FREDERIC. I'm sorry. Perhaps he went away because he saw me coming.
ISABELLE. No.
FREDERIC. Don't be unhappy. (*Sits* L. *of* ISABELLE *on steps.*) One unhappy person at a party is enough. I don't know how it is, but I should hate it if you were unhappy, too.
ISABELLE. Please let me alone.
FREDERIC. I want to tell you something; I realize it's no consolation to hear other people's troubles, but even so—it's something I've been almost certain about since yesterday. She wanted to be engaged to me because she couldn't be engaged to my brother. She said to herself, "If the other one won't marry me I'll take his double."
ISABELLE. If that were true it would be shameful.
FREDERIC. No; very lucky, really. Otherwise she would never have chosen me at all. Anyway, I'm used to it. When we were little, if my brother was naughty and the governess couldn't find him, she punished me. I was a sort of alternative. Life only comes to me absent-mindedly.
ISABELLE. You, as well.
FREDERIC. Why do you say "you as well"? You can't know what it feels like. (*Music ceases.* ISABELLE *rises, crosses below* FREDERIC, *stands with her back to him gazing off* D. L.) I don't mean to pay you an empty compliment, this is hardly the moment; but I'm certain no one could mistake you for anyone else. (ISABELLE *shakes her head to someone off* L., *then turns.*)
ISABELLE. It wasn't because of your brother that I was crying.
FREDERIC. No?
ISABELLE. It was because of you.
FREDERIC. (*Rising, moving* D. C.) Because of me?
ISABELLE. (*Easing* L. C.) Yes—Frederic, it's you I love.

47

FREDERIC. Oh! (*Crosses above* ISABELLE *and exits* L. C. *Music of a two-step commences off* L.)

ISABELLE. Oh! (*Runs across toward exit* D. R. HUGO *enters* D. L., *runs after* ISABELLE, *catches her by the hand.*)

HUGO. Very good! But you needn't have run away. That's the first time anyone has told him they loved him. (*Swings* ISABELLE *across to* L. *of him.*) You see, you've made him walk with quite a swagger. (ISABELLE *stands* R. *of steps.*) Let's make things even brisker. (*Sits on downstage chair.*) A pinch of jealousy while the blood's on the simmer. A third young man is in love with you.

ISABELLE. What young man?

HUGO. That's my business; I'll find one. Furious because I never leave your side, he challenges me to fight, and we choose our weapons.

ISABELLE. (*Moving* D. C.) You're mad!

HUGO. Imagine it. (*Rises.*) A duel by moonlight, in the spinney, during supper. Conversation disrupted by the sound of pistol shots. They stop the orchestra, (*Crosses below* ISABELLE *to* L. C.) and all troop into the park with lanterns and hurricane lamps to look for the corpse. And then you, your wits crazed with love—you do thoroughly understand you're crazed with love, don't you, Isabelle?—you jump into the lake. You swim, I imagine? Well, anyway, it doesn't matter; you've got feet, the lake's no depth, and I shall be there. I shall fish you out, drag you back to land, lay you streaming with water on the grass at my brother's feet, and say to him, "There! You did this!" And if he doesn't love you after that, he's got more resistance than I have. (*Pauses.*) You're looking rather dubious. Don't you enjoy bathing? I'll treble your fee. I'll buy you another dress. (*Suddenly takes her in his arms, speaks like a little spoilt boy.*) Come along now. (DIANA *enters* R. C., *moves to tree.*) Be a nice girl, agree to it, to please me. I'm enjoying myself so much tonight, and it's not often that I do.

ISABELLE. (*Breaking* D. R.) Oh! (*She exits* D. R.)

DIANA. (*Calling.*) Frederic.

HUGO. (*Turning with a smile.*) Hugo, if you please.

DIANA. (*Moving* C.) Oh! I beg your pardon.

HUGO. (*Easing to* L. *of* DIANA.) I'm not blushing. The one who doesn't blush is Hugo. Remember that: you may find it useful. Are you looking for him?

DIANA. I thought it was Frederic with that girl in his arms. As it was you, it's different. I apologize. Have you seen him?

HUGO. Of course. Everybody except you has seen him. He wanders like a soul in pain through this desert of gaiety. Why? (*Crosses below* DIANA *to* R. *of her.*) Are you wanting to satisfy yourself that you've well and truly broken his heart this evening?

DIANA. I don't want to break anyone's heart. It wouldn't amuse me at all. (*They start to dance two-step and continue with it while speaking.*) By the way, when I was in the park yesterday, one of you kissed me, and Frederic swears it wasn't him. (*They dance* D. L.) I lied so that he shouldn't be upset. But it must have been you. (HUGO *laughs. They turn and dance* D. R.) It's the kind of joke I detest.

HUGO. Yesterday? In the park? At what time?

DIANA. Don't pretend not to remember, Hugo. After dinner. (*They dance to* C.)

HUGO. After dinner? You've made a mistake, my dear. I was playing billiards with Patrice Bombelles.

DIANA. Frederic swears it wasn't him.

HUGO. I can only suppose it was yet another son of Adam, making the most of some vague resemblance to us.

DIANA. You're wrong to play with your brother's feelings, Hugo; it's too cruel. Even if you loved me, even if your love for me were too strong to control. But it isn't too strong to control, is it? (*They stop dancing,* HUGO L. *of* DIANA.)

HUGO. You put me in an impossible situation, Diana. I'm obliged to say "No." (*Kisses* DIANA'S *hand.*)

DIANA. (*Trying to box* HUGO'S *ear.*) I hate you! (HUGO *ducks and crosses below* DIANA *to* R. *of her.*)

HUGO. You, as well? I'm not very popular this evening. (*Moves above* DIANA, *speaks over her shoulder.*) Have you seen Patrice Bombelles? I gather he's looking everywhere for me. It's funny, but he didn't take to finding me in that little girl's arms, either. It seems he's mad about her. I didn't know, though I suppose I might have guessed, because everybody seems to be. (*Goes up on to rostrum.*) And I admit she's enchanting, and she's wearing a very pretty dress moreover. Don't you find it so? Well, good-bye. (*Moves to upstage end of rostrum.*) Shall I send Frederic to you?

DIANA. Thank you very much. I'll find him myself. (HUGO *exits*

49

U. R. *Music ceases.* DIANA *moves restlessly to tree, then looks off* L. *and calls.*) Father. (MESSERSCHMANN *enters* D. L.)

MESSERSCHMANN. (*As he enters.*) Well, dear?

DIANA. (*Moving* C.) Did you hear him? Did you hear how he was mocking me?

MESSERSCHMANN. (*Easing to* L. *of* DIANA.) No, I didn't.

DIANA. Really, things are going so wrong you'd think we had no money at all. Please be so good as to make me happy again, at once. (*Music of a Polka commences off* L.)

MESSERSCHMANN. But what is the matter, my darling? You said you wanted this boy Frederic and I bought him for you. Is he trying to get out of it?

DIANA. You didn't buy him for me; he loves me. But his brother is laughing at me.

MESSERSCHMANN. I can't give you both of them; not because I'm not rich enough, but it isn't the custom. Marry whichever you prefer.

DIANA. (*Moving on to steps.*) You're not rich enough to buy me the one I prefer. (*Leans against pillar* R. *of steps.*) That's why I took the other one.

MESSERSCHMANN. Not rich enough! Don't put me in a rage.

DIANA. Well, look what's happening to me, and it's Hugo who's making it happen, deliberately, I'm certain. I'm certain he brought this girl here, and she's trying to make Frederic lose interest in me; and Hugo, who never looks at anybody, the cold impersonal Hugo, never takes his eyes off her. I should begin to think I wasn't here, except that everyone has such an air of *not* looking at me that I know I must be. It's bad enough to be looked at as though you weren't there, but it's terrible, terrible, *not* to be looked at as though you were. So please set about making me happy again.

MESSERSCHMANN. (*Moving up steps and standing* L. *of her, thoughtfully.*) Who is this girl? (*Takes her hand.*) I can do almost nothing with a young girl.

DIANA. Romainville's niece.

MESSERSCHMANN. Which is Romainville?

DIANA. He's the one who looks as though he has gone on a horse to catch butterflies.

MESSERSCHMANN. But where does his money come from?

50

DIANA. He's a company director, like all the rest of the men here. (*They move* D. C.)

MESSERSCHMANN. What does he seem to be in? Steel, cement, potash, sulphates, zinc, aluminum, creosote, nuts, nickel, emulsion, tyres, *bijouterie*, sewing-machines, tunnels, rackets ——

DIANA. I think he said something about pig-iron.

MESSERSCHMANN. Pig-iron! Lead me to him. (*He moves, puts arm around* DIANA'S *shoulders, they move* D. L.) What do you want him to do, my darling girl? Do you want me to make him send her away at the height of the Ball?

DIANA. Oh—do you think you can?

MESSERSCHMANN. I've got them all in the palm of my hand. I lift a finger and their incomes are only half as much. (*Music ceases.*)

DIANA. I'm afraid it's impossible, Father.

MESSERSCHMANN. (*Calmly.*) If he has a ha'penny in pig-iron, nothing is impossible. (*Takes her by the hand, they exit* D. L. *Music of The Lancers commences off* L. PATRICE *enters* R. C., *crosses above conservatory, comes down rostrum, stands at top of steps.* HUGO *enters* D. R., *moves* C.)

HUGO. Sir!

PATRICE. Sir?

HUGO. I was looking for you.

PATRICE. For me?

HUGO. Yes. I have to speak to you.

PATRICE. About what?

HUGO. You were in the park yesterday, I think with Lady Dorothy India, my cousin?

PATRICE. Possibly.

HUGO. I noticed you. You seemed to be having a rather heated discussion.

PATRICE. On quite general matters, if I remember.

HUGO. I don't doubt it. But at one moment you must have out-generalled yourself; the lady slapped your face.

PATRICE. Mine, sir?

HUGO. This one.

PATRICE. (*Moving on to bottom step.*) You're mistaken, sir.

HUGO. No, sir.

PATRICE. That is to say, the lady may have struck me, but that's

51

no reason for you to think what you appear to be thinking, sir. (*Moves* L.)

HUGO. What do I appear to be thinking?

PATRICE. (*Turning his back on* HUGO.) After all, damn it, a slap on the cheek isn't always the sign of an understanding between a man and a woman.

HUGO. Certainly not.

PATRICE. (*Turning.*) One slaps the most casual acquaintances, even complete strangers. It signifies absolutely nothing. For instance, if I were suddenly to strike you now, would you deduce from this that we were on amorous terms?

HUGO. I'd protect myself from that to the death.

PATRICE. Then, may I ask, why you're trying to provoke me? (HUGO *shrugs shoulders, moves below chairs. Crosses to* L. *of* HUGO.) Winks, sighs, hints, unpleasant chuckles, which you try to camouflage with cigar-smoke. (*Taps* HUGO'S *back.* HUGO *crosses below* PATRICE *to* C. *He moves to* R. *of* HUGO.) You didn't fool me yesterday on the terrace; oh no, I wasn't fooled for a moment.

HUGO. (*Breaking* D. L.) You're very clairvoyant.

PATRICE. I can't go on with this a moment longer.

HUGO. (*Turning sharply to* PATRICE.) This is just what I wanted to make you say. (*Moves to* PATRICE, *leads him* D. R.) Let's talk it over quietly, like the nice fellows we are. Between you and me and the bedpost, this long-drawn-out affair with my mad cousin is boring you to desperation; admit it.

PATRICE. (*Breaking* D. R. C.) I've never said so.

HUGO. (*Moving in to* R. *of* PATRICE.) Naturally not. But let's speak frankly, shall we? You're in the hell of a cleft stick. If Messerschmann gets to know she's your mistress ——

PATRICE. (*Terrified.*) Don't say that, don't mention it.

HUGO. (*Gripping* PATRICE'S *throat.*) He'll break your neck.

PATRICE. (*Releasing himself, desperately.*) I've been enduring this for two years, twenty-four months—a hundred and four nerve-racking weeks, seven hundred and twenty-eight days ——

HUGO. (*Patting* PATRICE'S *cheek.*) Never mind, dear man; it will be all over this evening. (*Moves, sits on downstage chair.*)

PATRICE. (*Moving to* L. *of* HUGO.) What do you mean?

HUGO. In the simplest possible way. (*Pulls upstage chair to face him and taps it.* PATRICE *sits on chair, facing* HUGO.) Imagine you're on a visit to the dentist. You've rung the bell, flickered over the pages, of the magazines in the waiting-room, and now you're sitting in the dentist's chair. You've shown him the bad tooth; the dentist has seized the forceps. You're a big boy now; it's too late to run off home.

PATRICE. Do you know my dentist?

HUGO. No.

PATRICE. What are you talking about?

HUGO. This. Either you fall in with my plans this evening, or else, to be honest with you, I make quite sure that your employer knows how you employ yourself.

PATRICE. No!

HUGO. Now I wonder what you mean when you say "No"?

PATRICE. You're a gentleman, you wouldn't do it.

HUGO. Not by anonymous letters or by bribing a servant; but though I do things like a gentleman, I do them.

PATRICE. You're contemptible!

HUGO. I see.

PATRICE. And you're not ashamed?

HUGO. Not at all.

PATRICE. Oh. Then there's nothing more to discuss. What do you want me to do?

HUGO. This. I want you to choose the alternative way of having your neck broken. There's a very charming girl here tonight. It's a matter of the greatest importance, which I can't explain, that you pretend you're in love with her.

PATRICE. (*Rising.*) I?

HUGO. (*Rising.*) You. (*Moves toward* PATRICE.) But that's not all. (PATRICE *backs* D. L. C. *He follows* PATRICE.) You've seen me in the arms of this girl, and in a fit of ungovernable jealousy you box my ears.

PATRICE. I?

HUGO. You. (*Seizes* PATRICE'S *arm.*) Come with me. (*Drags* PATRICE U. L. *of conservatory, then across to* R.) We put the incident on a proper footing. We fight by moonlight, in the spinney, with pistols. (*Music ceases.*) Don't be afraid; I'm a very good shot. I promise I shan't hit you. (HUGO *and* PATRICE *exit* U. R. *Music of a waltz commences off* L. CAPULET *enters* R. C., *moves to* R. *of trellis, peers round it, then eases* D. C. MOTHER *enters* D. R., *crosses to* R. *of* CAPULET. MOTHER *is magnificently dressed and plumed.*)

53

CAPULET. Oh! Oh! You look like the best in the land, you do really, really you do.

MOTHER. Do I, Capulet?

CAPULET. Really you do! You couldn't look nicer in that dress if you'd been born in it.

MOTHER. It's my dreams come true, isn't it? (*Crosses below* CAPULET *to* L. C.) I feel as if I'd been born in it.

CAPULET. No one could doubt it. (*Moves* R.) But wait, wait. I'll go and find madame. (*Exits* R. C. MOTHER *waltzes dreamily in a small circle* L. C. JOSHUA *enters* D. L. *They collide.*)

MOTHER. } (*Together.*) } Oh!
JOSHUA. }

MOTHER. My man, would you kindly announce me? The Countess Funela.

JOSHUA. The Countess ——?

MOTHER. (*Magnificently.*) Funela.

JOSHUA. (*Crossing below* MOTHER *to exit* D. R.; *shouting.*) Mr. Hugo. Mr. Hugo. Help me, Mr. Hugo, sir. (*Exits* D. R. MOTHER *stands below steps.* MME. DESMORTES, *pushed by* CAPULET, *enters* R. C.)

MME. DESMORTES. (*Looking after* JOSHUA.) Where's he running? What is it? Fire? That would be most diverting. (MOTHER *curtsies.*) Let me see you, *ma chérie. Mille tonnerres!* Why, she's a great success. Now we'll go in and make a sensation. (CAPULET *pushes chair to* C. HUGO, *followed by* JOSHUA, *enters* D. R. JOSHUA *stands* U. R. *of chairs.* HUGO *moves to* R. C. CAPULET *turns chair to face* R.) My dear Hugo, I know you will be delighted to be presented to one of my oldest and dearest friends. The Countess Funela. We knew one another in Italy. (*To* MOTHER.) My nephew Hugo, Countess.

MOTHER. (*Crossing above* MME. DESMORTES *to* L. *of* HUGO.) I'm so charmed to meet you.

HUGO. Madame!

MME. DESMORTES. Come along, my dear. Wheel, Capulet. (CAPULET *wheels chair* D. L., *turns it to face front.* MOTHER *stands* L. *of chair,* CAPULET *above it.* HUGO *eases* C.) I'm so happy to see you again after such a desolation of separation. We can talk about Venice. Such days! Do you remember Palestrini? Such a madman. Jaundice made an end of him. Now shall I introduce you to all my other guests? (MOTHER *crosses below chair to* R. *of it.*) Tell me, my dear, you have a daughter, isn't that so? What has become of her?

MOTHER. Oh, it's a very long story indeed.

MME. DESMORTES. Well, you must let me hear it. We have all the night before us—haven't we, Hugo? (CAPULET *wheels* MME. DESMORTES *off* D. L. MOTHER *follows them off. Music ceases.* JOSHUA *eases* D. R. C. HUGO *moves to steps.*)

JOSHUA. (*Badly shaken.*) Here's the key, Mr. Hugo. (*Shows* HUGO *a key.*) So she can only have got out through the window, unless madame opened the door herself. When I heard her say the Countess Funela, I could have knocked myself down with one of her feathers. (*He so far forgets himself as to sit on upstage chair, but quickly rises.*) Oh, I beg your pardon, sir.

HUGO. (*Crossing to* L. *of* JOSHUA.) What for?

JOSHUA. I sat down. Quite an accident, sir. (HUGO *crosses to* R. *of chairs.*) That hasn't happened to me before in thirty years. (*Crosses below* HUGO *to* R. ROMAINVILLE *enters* U. L., *hurries* D. *to* L. *of* HUGO.)

ROMAINVILLE. (*As he enters.*) Stop! Oh, stop! Stop!

HUGO. Stop what?

ROMAINVILLE. Everything, stop everything. This time it's altogether calamitous. We've fallen into a trap, we're caught by the avalanche. (MESSERSCHMANN *enters* L. C., *stands* D. L. *of conservatory.*) High finance at its worst. Don't say a word about it. Isabelle must be got away this instant, this very moment, or else I'm ruined. (*Crosses below* HUGO *to* R. *of him.*)

HUGO. What in the world are you raving about? Everybody's out of their minds tonight.

ROMAINVILLE. I'm a director of several sulphate companies, and one pig-iron company.

HUGO. Yes, we know that. But what's that got to do with it?

ROMAINVILLE. That's why Isabelle must leave this house at once. Yes: powerful financial interests make it essential. Not a word. I can't explain. Manoeuvres at the Stock Exchange. (MESSERSCHMANN *exits* L. C.) If you won't help me, your aunt can go to the devil. (*Breaks* D. R., *bumps into* JOSHUA.) Oh, I'm so sorry. (*Moves to* R. *of* HUGO.) I'd sooner have the scandal. I'd sooner upset her for life. I'd sooner any damn thing. I'm going to tell her the whole truth immediately.

HUGO. Tell my aunt? (*Takes* ROMAINVILLE *by shoulders, puts him across to* C.) Just take a look at who she's introducing to every-body, in the middle of the ballroom.

ROMAINVILLE. (*Peering off* L.) I'm too short-sighted. I can't see at this distance.

HUGO. (*Crossing* D. L.) Put your glasses on; it's worth it.

ROMAINVILLE. (*Putting on his glasses, looking off* L.) Good Heavens! (*Moves* L. C.) What on earth is she doing? Am I dream-ing or is that ——

HUGO. Yes. The Countess Funela. She used to revolve in the best Italian circles.

ROMAINVILLE. Is this you up to your tricks again?

HUGO. No. But my aunt is up to hers.

ROMAINVILLE. But why?

HUGO. No reason, which is what makes it serious. (*Music of a two-step commences off* L. PATRICE *enters aggressively* D. R. *Carries a pair of gloves.*)

PATRICE. (*Moving* C.) Sir! (HUGO, *having forgotten his plan with* PATRICE, *answers absent-mindedly.*)

HUGO. Sir? (PATRICE *clicks his heels, bows, then strides to* R. *of* HUGO.)

PATRICE. This state of affairs cannot go on, and as you refuse to give the girl up —— (*Tries to slap* HUGO'S *face with his gloves.*)

HUGO. (*Pushing* PATRICE *away, impatiently.*) No, no, no! Another time. (PATRICE *recoils to* C.) You're being a nuisance. Later on, later on. (*Grabs* ROMAINVILLE *by hand, drags him in a flurry up on to rostrum.*) Come on, Romainville; we've got to go and stop her jumping in the lake. (*Crosses above conservatory, exits* U. R., *dragging* ROMAINVILLE *with him.*)

PATRICE. All right. I'll come back. (*Crosses to exit* D. R., *bumps into* JOSHUA, *mutters apology, exits. As he does so,* MOTHER *and* GENERAL *enter* D. L., *dancing two-step. They dance to exit* D. R. *and bump into* JOSHUA *who reels* U. R. C. CAPULET *wheels* MME. DESMORTES *on briskly* D. L. MOTHER *and* GENERAL *dance off* D. R. CAPULET *swings chair in a complete circle* C., *then pushes it off* D. R. JOSHUA *reels to* L. C., *then exits* D. L.)

CURTAIN

ACT III

SCENE 1

SCENE: *The same. The same evening. After supper.*
Trellis R. C., *flower-bed and two chairs are removed.*
Three small supper tables are set, one U. C., *one* R. C.,
with chairs R. *and* L. *of it, and one* D. R., *also with chairs*
R. *and* L. *of it. White cloths with remains of supper are*
still on tables. When curtain rises ISABELLE *is seated* R.
of table D. R. HUGO *stands on top step. He is smoking*
a cigar in a holder.

ISABELLE. And so?

HUGO. And so it doesn't amuse me any more. (*Moves* C.) And
anyway that moronic mother of yours is going to drop every brick
in the hod any moment now. (ISABELLE *buries face in her hands.*)
Look at her: cooing and clucking and crowing, all our feathered
friends rolled into one. (*Moves above table* R. C.) She makes me
shiver. She told General de Saint-Mouton that she's the Pope's
god-daughter. He's delighted; he can see his catholicism becoming
profitable at last; he imagines he's Ambassador to the Vatican
already.

ISABELLE. (*Looking up.*) Am I still to throw myself into the lake?

HUGO. That's no good now; we must think of something better,
and think quickly, or else my respectable undelectable aunt is
quite likely to spoil the whole thing. (*Pauses.*) I know! I've got it.

ISABELLE. You frighten me when you say that.

HUGO. There's no doubt you're still the attraction of the evening.
You've made a sensation, in spite of your mother behaving like a
circus. Distinction, poise, reserve—even the dowagers are on your
side.

"What birdwings rocked her cradle, what swift grace
 Caught her and taught her limbs to move
Gravely as shadows in a sunlit place,
 Or branches in a grove?"
I walk behind you, gleaning the whispers, as flattered as if I were

57

an impresario. (*Moves* D. C.) Your effect on the men needs no comment. But all the mothers with marriageable daughters have shot their lorgnettes at you; and you emerge unscathed. You return triumphant from the underworld of undertones. And the daughters are white with fury. (*Moves to* L. *of table* D. R.) Where Diana fell they tumble after. But all this is only a curtain-raiser, (*Stubs out his cigar in ash-tray on table* D. R.) an appetizer, good enough to revive poor Frederic. Now I'm ready for better things. (*Perches himself on* L. *side of table* D. R.) I'm going to start a rumor that you're not Romainville's niece at all, nor can your mother possibly be your mother. Better still, you're the wonderfully wealthy side-issue of a Portuguese princess and an Admiral, an Admiral who wrote Byronic poetry and was drowned at sea— I shall think of one; there must have been several—and this is your coming-out party, incognito. And in the small hours, when my little puffball of a story has been blown sufficiently from mouth to mouth, when my cuckoo-history has laid its eggs in the well-washed ears of all the little ladies, when Diana is withered with jealousy, when my abstracted brother, vaguely flattered by your smiling on him, has begun to look not quite so submissively at his executioner, I shall step from the wings, climb on a chair as though to announce the Cotillion, crave silence, and say to them more or less: "My lords, ladies and gentlemen, you've been cuckooed!" And, making the most of the confusion, I shall continue: "Dear asses. Tonight has been all a gullery; a fiction, all of it. Conceived and planned, and carried out to the letter. (*Rises.*) During these few memorable hours you've been able to see"—I shall say, calling on Diana to witness it—"into the hearts of these young ladies: the rocks that lie there, the sediment, the dead flowers. And you have also been able to see"—and here my gesture will light on you—"something too like an angel to be true. You've been made dupes of, ladies and gentlemen. What you have called distinction, breeding, poise, are only pretences. This angel, this girl who made your evening dazzle, is a lay-figure hired by me, a poor little ballet dancer from the Opera brought here to play the part. She's not Romainville's niece, and she's not the daughter of any Byronic Admiral: she is nothing at all. And no one would have more than barely noticed her if I'd brought her here to do her usual turn." (*Stands on chair* L. *of table* D. R.) "But her turn tonight has been to represent yourselves. I've brought her here, thrown her amongst you, dressed by your own dress-maker, using the words of your own kind, and this has been enough to knock sideways for a whole evening the prestige of your society beauty. 'Vanity, vanity, all is vanity.' I hope at least that my brother Frederic now sees the light. As for me, I find you unutterably dreary. I should be glad to have looked my last on the whole lot of you. Tomorrow I set off by the first train to hunt big game in Africa." How do you like that, Isabelle?

ISABELLE. (*After pause, softly.*) What happens to me?

HUGO. You? What do you mean?

ISABELLE. I mean, what becomes of me?

HUGO. (*Stepping down from chair, moving above table* D. R.) What do you want to become of you? You go off home, with the present you well deserve, with your mother on your arm and you on Romainville's; and you have a nice dress and a happy memory. Nothing more than that ever remains of a night's dancing.

ISABELLE. You haven't thought I might be ashamed?

HUGO. Of what? You're a free spirit, and intelligent. You must loathe all these people, as much as I do. Together we're going to have a good laugh at them. What better entertainment? You wouldn't want to be *like* them, would you?

ISABELLE. No, but—give the dress to someone else, and let me go home. I'll call my mother; you can send us back to St. Fleur *now*, and I promise no one will hear of me again.

HUGO. (*Crossing* D. L. C.) Nonsense!

ISABELLE. (*Rising, crossing to* L. *of* HUGO.) It may be, but—not in front of your brother, then. Nor in front of you. Not just yet.

HUGO. (*Crossing below* ISABELLE *to* L. *of her.*) Yes, now. This moment.

ISABELLE. It's wrong to think only of how it's going to amuse you.

HUGO. It's all there's time for, before we laugh on the other side of our graves. (*Exits* D. L. ISABELLE *leans against downstage jalousie, with a little hurt cry.* DIANA *enters* R. C., *moves to* L. *of table* R. C. *Stands for a moment looking at* ISABELLE, *who raises her head after a moment and sees* DIANA.)

DIANA. It's quite true; you're wearing a most attractive dress.

ISABELLE. (*Moving* L. C.) Yes, it is.

DIANA. (*Moving to* R. *of* ISABELLE.) And you're looking beautiful; that's true, too.

ISABELLE. Thank you. (DIANA *moves above* ISABELLE, *inspecting her, then goes up steps.* ISABELLE *eases* C.)

DIANA. Perhaps not perfectly groomed, still a little too close to nature; and certainly not a very good powder, nor a very good perfume.

ISABELLE. That must be why I find yours a little too good, and you a little too far ——

DIANA. Well? Too far what?

ISABELLE. —from nature.

DIANA. (*Crossing below* ISABELLE.) You've managed quite well; (*Moves below table* D. R.) but if one hasn't a maid who understands these things it's almost fatal; with the best will in the world one neglects oneself. No woman can tend herself and altogether survive. Do you get up early in the morning?

ISABELLE. (*Moving to* L. *of* DIANA.) Yes.

DIANA. Yes, one can see.

ISABELLE. Do you go late to bed?

DIANA. Yes.

ISABELLE. Yes, one can see.

DIANA. (*After slight pause.*) Tell me, do you mind very much?

ISABELLE. Mind what?

DIANA. Wearing something you haven't made yourself?

ISABELLE. As a compensation, my eyelashes are my own.

DIANA. Happily for you. You'll need them tomorrow, without the help you get from the dress.

ISABELLE. I take it away with me. It was given me.

DIANA. That's very nice, isn't it? You'll be able to be a beauty all over again. I hear they're holding a jolly dance on the fourteenth day of July at St. Fleur. You'll turn all the bumpkins' heads. (*Crosses below* ISABELLE *to* C.) Do you like my dress?

ISABELLE. Yes, it's most beautiful.

DIANA. Would you like it? I shall never wear it again. I hardly ever wear a dress more than once. Besides, I can't really tell myself I like petunia. Tomorrow I shall dine in rose-pink, rather a miracle dress, a harness of little pleats, twenty yards of them. If you come up to my room I'll show it to you. (*Takes* ISABELLE *by hand, draws her* L. C.) Yes, do come and see it; I'm sure it'll give you pleasure.

ISABELLE. (*Withdrawing her hand.*) No. (*Backs to* L. *of table* D. R.)

DIANA. Why not? Do you envy me? That's one of the sins, you know. You'd love to be rich, wouldn't you? If this evening were only a true story, and you had as many dresses as I have.

ISABELLE. Naturally.

DIANA. But you'll never have more than one, isn't that so? (ISABELLE *turns, moves above able* D. R., *toward exit* R. C. *She moves quickly to* L. *of* ISABELLE.) And if I put my foot on your train (*Puts her foot on hem of* ISABELLE'S *frock.*) in this way— (ISABELLE *stops and turns.*)—and tug it a little, you'll not even have one.

ISABELLE. Take your foot away.

DIANA. No.

ISABELLE. Take your foot away or else I shall hit you.

DIANA. Don't squirm, you little fury; you'll do some damage. (ISABELLE *pulls at frock and it tears.*)

ISABELLE. (*With a cry.*) Oh! My dress!

DIANA. You did it yourself. (*Moves* L. *of table* U. C.) A few tacks, it will still do very nicely for St. Fleur. It's exciting, I expect, to have such a triumphant evening with a borrowed dress on your back. The pity is, it's over so soon. Tomorrow morning you have to pack your cardboard box, and I shall still be here, and that's the difference between us. (*Pours a glass of champagne for herself, goes up steps, leans against post* R. *of them. A short pause.* ISABELLE *looks at* DIANA, *but without dislike.*)

ISABELLE. (*Suddenly.*) Is it so pleasant to be unpleasant? (*Moves below table* U. C.)

DIANA. (*With a change of tone, sighing.*) No. But one can't always be pleased.

ISABELLE. Can you be unhappy as well? That's very strange. Why?

DIANA. I have too much money.

ISABELLE. But Frederic loves you.

DIANA. I don't love him. I love Hugo, and he dislikes my money, and I think he's right.

ISABELLE. Become poor, then.

DIANA. Do you think it is so easy?

ISABELLE. (*Easing* D. C.) I make no effort.

DIANA. (*Crossing to table* D. R.) You don't know how lucky you are. (*Puts her glass on table.*) I suppose this is a lovely party— but all my friends give parties like it. (*Moves to* R. *of table* D. R.)

61

I shall never again know the excitement of being invited up to the great house—and that's so sad.

ISABELLE. So sad.

DIANA. I tell you money is only worth something to the poor.

ISABELLE. Which proves there is something the matter with the world. I have been humiliated and hurt this evening, and my only dress has been torn, because I'm one of the poor ones. (*Moves above chair* L. *of table* D. R.) I'm going to do what the poor ones always do. I'm leaving words for deeds, and asking you to go away.

DIANA. (*Sitting* R. *of table* D. R.) Go away? Do you think you're in your own home, you little adventuress?

ISABELLE. Go and cry over your millions somewhere a long way off. I'm pretty stupid and very ashamed to have spent so many minutes trying to understand you. So now I shall use the arguments of the poor. (*Moves below table* D. R.) If you don't go I shall throw you out.

DIANA. Throw me out? I should like to see you try.

ISABELLE. You're going to see me try. And as you wouldn't care if I tore your dress, I shall tear your face instead: God has been unusually impartial, giving us one face each. (*Grabs* DIANA *by the hair.*)

DIANA. (*Rising.*) You're a common little slut. Do you think I'm afraid? (*Kicks her chair away and with* ISABELLE *still hanging on to her hair, backs above table* D. R. *to* R. C., *drawing* ISABELLE *with her.*)

ISABELLE. Not yet. But I think you may be.

DIANA. Oh! You'll ruin my hair.

ISABELLE. (*Pulling* DIANA'S *hair down.*) You have a maid to put it right. What does it matter? (*Releases* DIANA, *backs* D. R.)

DIANA. I've got claws as well as you.

ISABELLE. (*Rushing at* DIANA.) Then use them. (DIANA *seizes* ISABELLE'S *wrists, swings her round to* C.)

DIANA. I was poor once, myself. (*Stamps on* ISABELLE'S R. *foot with her* L. ISABELLE *yelps and breaks* D. L. C.) When I was ten I fought all the little toughs on the docks at Istanboul. (ISABELLE *runs at* DIANA, *there is a sharp tussle in which they box each other's ears, and* DIANA *pulls* ISABELLE'S *hair down. As they wrestle together,* JOSHUA *enters* R. C. *As he sees them he gives a yell of horror, crosses quickly, exits* D. L.)

JOSHUA. (*As he exits, calling.*) Mr. Hugo! Mr. Hugo! (DIANA *throws* ISABELLE *to the ground, picks up remains of some fruit from the table* U. C., *throws it over* ISABELLE, *then collapses* L. *of her on the ground.* FREDERIC *enters* D. L., *stands speechless with his back to audience.* DIANA *rises, moves below table* D. R. *to* R. *of it.*)

ISABELLE. (*Mistaking* FREDERIC *for* HUGO.) Well, are you satisfied now? Don't you think you've had a great success? (*Gets to her knees.*) You wanted entertainment, and no one can say you haven't had it. (*Rises, moves* C.) How is this for your scandal? You stood up on your chair and told them who I was: or if you haven't yet, you have no need to. I'm going to show myself to them, looking as I am. A common little slut, as this lady called me. You can watch your bit of fun get funnier. They'll have no doubts about me now; they'll know exactly where I come from. Do you want me to tell you the climax of the Ball? To begin with, I insult my mother: I pluck her feathers in front of them all: and I take her away, back to her piano lessons. Down the wind goes the Countess Funela. Her father sold wallpaper: he carried the rolls on his back and a paste-pot in his hand. They used to give him five francs a time, which kept him happy because it meant he could buy himself a drink without telling his wife. (DIANA *eases above table* D. R.) That's the poor for you. You wanted to play with them tonight because you were bored, but you'll see what a mistake it was, and how right your nurses were when you were little and told you not to play with the common children in the park. They don't know how to play, and I haven't played for one moment since I came here. I've been unhappy: isn't that vulgar of me? I've been unhappy. And all because you didn't understand, or wouldn't understand, that I love you. (DIANA *eases above* ISABELLE *to* U. L. *of* FREDERIC.) It's because I love you that I've done my best to dazzle them this evening; it's because I love you that I've pretended to love your brother; it's because I love you that I was ready to throw myself in the lake, like a baby and a fool, to finish it all. If I hadn't loved you, and loved you from the moment we met, do you think I should have agreed to be in your mad puppet show? (*Pauses.*) Well, won't you say something? It's tiresome, of course, this poor girl standing here saying she loves you. But please say *something*. You usually say so much. What's the matter?

FREDERIC. (*Stammering.*) But—I'm afraid—none of this was me.

ISABELLE. What do you mean, not me?

DIANA. (*Moving to* R. *of* FREDERIC, *linking her arm in his.*) Certainly it wasn't. Look at him. He's blushing: it's his brother.

ISABELLE. (*Suddenly confused.*) Oh, I'm so sorry—I'm so very sorry.

FREDERIC. No, no, no! (*Crosses below* DIANA *to* L. *of* ISABELLE.) It's I who should be sorry. I should have ——

DIANA. Come away, Frederic. There's nothing you need say to this girl. Hugo will send Joshua along to pay her, and she can go home.

FREDERIC. Don't talk like that, Diana.

DIANA. You will come with me now, Frederic, at once, or from now on you can stay away from me. (*Turns abruptly, exits* D. L.)

FREDERIC. I came to tell you how distressed I am by what you've been made to go through this evening, how unpleasant and cruel I know it has been. May I ask you to accept my most sincere apologies for all the rest of them here?

ISABELLE. (*Gently.*) You must go. If you don't follow her quickly, she's going to make you very wretched.

FREDERIC. (*Bowing.*) Will you excuse me, then? (*Moves to door* D. L., *then stops and turns.*) Shall I explain to my brother that you've told me you love him?

ISABELLE. No; there's no need. (FREDERIC *makes sorrowful gesture, exits* D. L. *A clock off is heard to strike three.* ISABELLE *moves* D. R., *picks up chair, replaces it* R. *of table* D. R. MOTHER *enters* D. L.)

MOTHER. (*Crossing to* L. *of table* D. R.) Oh, my dear child. Such mortification!

ISABELLE. (*Moving above table* D. R. *to* L. *to* MOTHER.) I was coming to find you.

MOTHER. (*Sinking on to chair* L. *of table* D. R.) Everything has collapsed. The young man has gone mad. He got up on to a chair, and said simply terrible things. There must be something really very wrong with his head. It's most unfortunate. If he had only waited for another hour I should have been spending the autumn with a General. A very nice one. But now everybody will turn their backs on me, I know they will.

ISABELLE. We're leaving now, Mother. Take off your finery. You have to give your piano lessons again next week.

MOTHER. You're quite extraordinary. There's not an ounce of poetry in you. All our brilliant dreams vanish, and you go on as usual. You're so insensitive. He couldn't have loved you, I suppose, and I was so convinced. (*Pauses.*) Well, why, why should he have asked you here if he wasn't in love with you?

ISABELLE. You've talked quite enough. (*Crosses below* MOTHER *to* D. R. *of her, holds* MOTHER'S R. *hand.*) Go and take off your feathers.

MOTHER. (*Rising.*) Now just listen to me. I've had a long conversation with Romainville. All this business this evening has nudged him awake, and he's spoken up at last. (ISABELLE *releases* MOTHER'S *hand, crosses below her to* R. C.) You've seen yourself this evening how the high-flown young men behave. (*Crosses to* L. *of* ISABELLE.) Romainville is middle-aged, steady, and a gentleman. He has had his eye on you for a long time, he told me so himself: he knows just what he can expect. He isn't going into it with his eyes shut. So there you are. He'll see we're both taken good care of; moreover, he hasn't actually said, but I know he means, that when he has talked his family round he may even make a promise to marry you. (ISABELLE *turns her back to* MOTHER.) Isn't that a nice surprise, dear?

ISABELLE. (*Breaking* D. R.) Now go upstairs.

MOTHER. (*Turning, moving toward exit* D. L.; *furiously.*) All right, then; go your own way; never think of me and all I've done for you. Lose a good chance, you stupid little ninny—(MESSERSCHMANN *enters* D. L.)—and lose your looks, too, before they get you anywhere. (*Turns and sees* MESSERSCHMANN. *Suddenly all smiles.*) Oh, I'm so happy to see you. How do you do?

MESSERSCHMANN. (*Coldly.*) Well, madam.

MOTHER. The Countess Funela. We were introduced just now, but in such a hubbub ——

MESSERSCHMANN. Madam, I must ask you to let me have a few moments alone with your daughter.

MOTHER. But of course you may. (ISABELLE *eases* C.) I give you my permission without any hesitation at all. (*Turns to* ISABELLE.) I'm leaving you with Mr. Messerschmann now, Isabelle. I'm going upstairs for a little rest. (*To* MESSERSCHMANN.) These social occasions, you know, are so tiring. One comes to wish for a little peace and quiet. (*Crosses below* ISABELLE *to* R. *of her.*) We go out too much, I'm afraid, a great deal too much. I'll leave you.

Don't forget about our good friend, Isabelle. (*Moves to exit* D. R.) We must give him an answer tonight, you know (*Stops and turns.*) to his charming invitation for the summer. (*Curtsies to* MESSERSCHMANN.) Dear sir, I'm delighted to have seen you again. Delighted! (*Exits* D. R. MESSERSCHMANN *crosses to* L. *of* ISABELLE.)

MESSERSCHMANN. (*Bluntly.*) Now, young lady, I'm going to be rather brutal. I know who you are, and in half an hour's time everybody will know. The party's over, as far as you're concerned. You've had a great success, everybody's been charmed by you, but it was a little adventure which couldn't last. I've come to ask you to cut it even shorter. Go up to your room, and disappear without seeing anyone again. (*Crosses below* ISABELLE *to* R. *of table* D. R.) And I shall be most grateful to you.

ISABELLE. (*Moving* D. C.) How can it affect you whether I go or stay?

MESSERSCHMANN. It's a little present I should like to give my daughter. You see, I make no bones about it. I've never deceived anyone in my business affairs, and I've always succeeded. (*Sits* R. *of table* D. R.) How much do you want?

ISABELLE. Nothing. I had decided to go before you asked me.

MESSERSCHMANN. I know. But it isn't fair that you should go without being paid. How much did Hugo promise you?

ISABELLE. My usual dancing fee, and this dress, which someone has torn.

MESSERSCHMANN. Who tore it?

ISABELLE. Your daughter.

MESSERSCHMANN. Then that's my business, too. As well as what you were going to ask me, I'll pay for two more dresses.

ISABELLE. Thank you, but I'm happy with this one, with the tear.

MESSERSCHMANN. Let's get the situation clear. I don't want you to see Hugo again, even to get your fee. How much do I pay you to go without seeing him?

ISABELLE. Nothing at all. I didn't expect to see him.

MESSERSCHMANN. But how about the money he promised you?

ISABELLE. I don't intend to take it. I can be said to have danced here this evening for my own pleasure. (MESSERSCHMANN *looks at her a moment in silence, then weightily and powerfully points to chair* L. *of table at which he sits.*)

MESSERSCHMANN. I don't like it when things don't cost anything, young lady.

ISABELLE. (*Sitting* L. *of* table D. R., *facing* MESSERSCHMANN.)
Does it disturb you?

MESSERSCHMANN. It's too expensive. Why are you refusing Hugo's
money?

ISABELLE. Because I'm glad not to take it.

MESSERSCHMANN. And mine?

ISABELLE. Because you haven't any reason to give it to me. I was
asked to act in a comedy here this evening. My performance is
over, the curtain is down, and I'm going home.

MESSERSCHMANN. But not with nothing to show for it?

ISABELLE. Why not?

MESSERSCHMANN. It's not as it should be.

ISABELLE. I'm sorry, but it's what I'm going to do. (*Rises, moves*
C.) You will excuse me.

MESSERSCHMANN. (*Angrily.*) No, no, no! Don't be like Ossowitch.

ISABELLE. (*Turning, astonished.*) Like Ossowitch?

MESSERSCHMANN. Yes. He was a banker of a rival group, and I
had to have important discussions with him. I never met such a
man for getting up and going. Whenever we disagreed, which was
pretty often, he got up and went. Every time I had to catch up
with him in the vestibule or in the lift or somewhere. And the
farther I had to go to catch him, the more it cost me. (*Rises,
moves to* R. *of* ISABELLE.) In the end I had to invite him to come
out in a canoe, when I'd first made quite sure he couldn't swim.
After that we were wonderfully good friends: but now he has
learnt to swim and things are not so nice. So don't you start this
getting up and going, my dear child, it isn't a good way to talk.
Nobody ever agrees with anybody in a business discussion, but
we stay sitting, or else business is no good. (*Takes* ISABELLE *by
arm, leads her to chair* L. *of table* D. R., *sits her on it.*) Now, come
along, my dear young lady, be reasonable. (*Eases above table*
D. R.) Strike a good bargain with me before it's too late. How
much do you want?

ISABELLE. Nothing.

MESSERSCHMANN. It's too much. Now, look, I'm going to be fool-
ish. I'm going to offer you twice what you expect. I've the notes
on me here. I always carry plenty of notes. (*Takes a bundle of
notes from his pocket.*) Look at this bundle here, such virgins and
so clean, such a pretty little bunch. It would be very nice, you

will agree with me, to carry about a sprig or two of these little papers?

ISABELLE. How should I carry them?

MESSERSCHMANN. Would you like me to wrap them up for you? I could make you a nice little parcel of them.

ISABELLE. Listen. I don't want to have to walk out like Mr. Ossowitch; I don't want to bring back unhappy memories to you; but I insist that you believe me. I don't want your money. (MESSERSCHMANN *replaces notes in pocket, breaks angrily* D. R. *then turns, crosses below* ISABELLE *to* C.)

MESSERSCHMANN. (*Angrily.*) You're being very exorbitant.

ISABELLE. Is it really possible to be a great power in the world without being very intelligent?

MESSERSCHMANN. I am intelligent. I'm very intelligent. It's because I'm very intelligent and experienced that I tell you I don't believe you.

ISABELLE. (*Rising, moving to* R. *of* MESSERSCHMANN, *taking him gently by arm.*) Then, if you're intelligent, let's talk intelligently. If you hadn't kept me here I should have been gone already. So you see I have nothing to sell.

MESSERSCHMANN. (*Angrily.*) There's always something to sell. Anyway, even if you haven't, I've got to buy something now we've started bargaining.

ISABELLE. Why?

MESSERSCHMANN. Why? Because I should lose all faith in myself if I didn't.

ISABELLE. (*With a little smile.*) If it takes so little to make you lose faith, I must write to Mr. Ossowitch.

MESSERSCHMANN. (*Deliberately.*) Ossowitch was a baby. (*Turns, faces* ISABELLE, *who retreats* D. R. MESSERSCHMANN *follows her closely all the way until* ISABELLE *is leaning against downstage side of table* D. R. *with* MESSERSCHMANN *standing over her.*) But you're an opponent who interests me. What I'm buying from you now isn't my daughter's peace of mind any more, it's my own peace of mind. And I put no limit whatsoever on that. How much do you want?

ISABELLE. Do men become masters of the world by continually repeating themselves?

MESSERSCHMANN. (*Breaking* L. C.) I'll make you as rich as any girl in the house tonight. (ISABELLE *crosses slowly to* L. *of him.*)

And if I want it, Romainville shall adopt you: you really will be his niece.

ISABELLE. (*Moving* D. L.) Thank you.

MESSERSCHMANN. Listen: I'll make you so rich, the grandest and handsomest young fellow here will ask you to marry him immediately.

ISABELLE. I'm sorry. But none of that will please me as much as saying "No" to you.

MESSERSCHMANN. (*Moving to steps, waving hands angrily above his head.*) Whatever shall I do? I don't believe in money any more either. All it gives me is dust, smoke, nausea and indigestion. I eat noodles and I drink water, and I get no pleasure at all from my frozen snow-queen mistress: I don't even suffer when she deceives me, because I don't really want her: I want nothing at all. (*Collapses, sits mournfully on* L. *end of steps.*) I'm a poor little tailor from Cracow, and my only really pleasant memory is the first suit I made when I was sixteen—(ISABELLE *moves slowly to* L. *of him.*)—a jacket for a priest, and it turned out very well. My father said to me: "This time you have done it well; you know now what your calling is." And I was happy—but since then I've succeeded at nothing, except at making money, more and more money, and money has never made anybody love me, not even my own daughter. (*Looks up at* ISABELLE.) Please be sympathetic. Do stand by me this evening. Take my money.

ISABELLE. No.

MESSERSCHMANN. No? Ah, well: now you can see what I'll do with these beautiful little bundles which can't do anything. (*Takes large bundle of notes from pocket, rises, moves* D. C.) I'll bite them and tear them with my teeth and spit them on the ground. (*Starts tearing notes with his teeth, then, for the sake of speed, with his hands.*)

ISABELLE. (*Moving to* L. *of* MESSERSCHMANN; *joyfully.*) What a good idea! Give me some, I'll help you. This will make me feel much better. (*Takes some of notes, starts happily and quietly to tear them into small pieces. Both throw scraps of paper into the air and work feverishly in a rain of paper.*)

MESSERSCHMANN. (*Ecstatically.*) There! So! So! There! So! That's a country house: the dream of all the small householders. (*Moves to* L. *of table* D. R.)

69

ISABELLE. (*Tearing merrily.*) With the garden, the pond, the gold-fish, the roses.

MESSERSCHMANN. Everything! There goes a business. A millinery business: the one I was going to give you, like the fool I was.

ISABELLE. Hooray! That was a hat.

MESSERSCHMANN. (*Still tearing, annoyed.*) Why only one hat?

ISABELLE. It was very expensive. (ISABELLE *crosses* D. R. MESSERSCHMANN *takes more notes from his pocket, drops them on floor* D. C. ISABELLE *moves to* R. *of him. Both kneel and proceed with destruction of notes.*)

MESSERSCHMANN. There goes the dresses, and still more dresses, rolls and folds and billows of material, what they're all dying to put on their backs. There go the cloaks and the coats and the wraps and the furs.

ISABELLE. (*Tearing.*) Not too many: it's nearly summer time.

MESSERSCHMANN. (*Tearing some notes, tossing pieces into the air.*) Away goes the beautiful line, the satin sheets, petticoats as light as cobwebs, embroidered handkerchieves.

ISABELLE. (*Tearing one note.*) There goes a trunk.

MESSERSCHMANN. (*Stopping in surprise.*) Why a trunk?

ISABELLE. To put everything into. (*Rises, crosses above* MESSERSCHMANN, *moves* D. L., *still tearing and throwing pieces into the air.*)

MESSERSCHMANN. (*Tearing.*) There go the necklaces, the bracelets, the rings—all the rings.

ISABELLE. (*Tearing one note.*) Oh! Such a beautiful pearl. (*Moves in to* L. *of* MESSERSCHMANN, *sits on the ground.*)

MESSERSCHMANN. You'll regret that.

ISABELLE. (*Taking another handful of notes.*) No, not a bit.

MESSERSCHMANN. Away go the holidays abroad, the servants, the racehorses, the beautiful ladies ready and willing, away go the consciences of honest men, and all the prosperity of this lamentable world. There! There! There! There! (*Tears last of notes, collapses on to* ISABELLE.) Are you happy now?

ISABELLE. (*Softly.*) No. Are you?

MESSERSCHMANN. Not at all. (*They kneel side by side, exhausted.* ISABELLE *finds one untorn note on ground, tears it up.*)

ISABELLE. There go the poor. We'd forgotten them. (*Pauses, looks at* MESSERSCHMANN. *Gently.*) I bet it wasn't so exhausting to get it all.

MESSERSCHMANN. I'm very unhappy.

ISABELLE. (*With a wry smile.*) Me too.

MESSERSCHMANN. I understand very well how you feel. And I'm the only person in this house this evening who does understand. For a long time, such a long time, I was humiliated, until I became stronger than they were. Then I could turn the tables. Every man is quite alone. That's definite. No one can help anyone else: he can only go on. (JOSHUA *enters* D. L., *stands gazing in surprise.* *To* JOSHUA.) What do you want?

JOSHUA. It's Mr. Hugo, sir: he wishes to speak to the young lady in the little drawing-room, to settle her account.

ISABELLE. (*Rising, crossing below* MESSERSCHMANN *to* R. *of him.*) Tell him he doesn't owe me anything. Mr. Messerschmann has paid me. (*Exits* R. C. MESSERSCHMANN *beckons to* JOSHUA, *who moves in to* L. *of him.*)

MESSERSCHMANN. My friend.

JOSHUA. Sir?

MESSERSCHMANN. You seem to have a pleasant face.

JOSHUA. (*After pause, astonished.*) I belong to a generation of old servants who could never permit themselves to have such a thing while on duty, sir. But on Sundays, and particularly on holidays, my friends tell me I have an amiable face, sir, almost jovial, and what I may call a nice face, very French and very homely, sir.

MESSERSCHMANN. Then listen to me. You must have read your Bible when you were a little boy?

JOSHUA. Here and there, sir, like everybody else.

MESSERSCHMANN. Did you ever come across Samson?

JOSHUA. (*Assisting* MESSERSCHMANN *to rise.*) The gentleman who had his hair cut, sir?

MESSERSCHMANN. Yes; and he was very unhappy. Jeered at, my friend, always jeered at by everybody. They had put his eyes out. They thought he was blind, but I'm sure he could see.

JOSHUA. Quite possible, sir.

MESSERSCHMANN. And then, one fine day, unable to stand it any more, he got them to lead him between the pillars of the temple. He was very strong, terribly strong, you understand? He twined his arms round the pillars—(*Puts his arms around* JOSHUA.) like this.

71

JOSHUA. (*Embarrassed.*) Oh! sir! Do take care, sir, someone will see us.

MESSERSCHMANN. And then he shook them with all his might. (*Shakes* JOSHUA.)

JOSHUA. (*As* MESSERSCHMANN *shakes him.*) Yes, sir. Do be careful, sir. I'm the one who will get into trouble. (MESSERSCHMANN, *his feelings relieved, releases* JOSHUA.)

MESSERSCHMANN. (*With a sigh.*) There!

JOSHUA. (*Adjusting his coat.*) Well, there, sir. It wasn't at all the thing to do in a church.

MESSERSCHMANN. (*With a chuckle.*) You might well say so. He was so strong the entire temple crushed down on to the two thousand Philistines who were there praying to their false Gods (*Crosses below* JOSHUA *to* L.) and thinking Samson no better than a fool.

JOSHUA. But it fell on him, too, sir.

MESSERSCHMANN. But that wasn't of any kind of importance. How could being poor hurt him?

JOSHUA. If you say so, sir. (*A pause.* JOSHUA *turns, moves toward exit* D. R.)

MESSERSCHMANN. My friend.

JOSHUA. (*Stopping, turning.*) Sir?

MESSERSCHMANN. (*Moving* C.) I'm putting through an overseas telephone call from my room tonight.

JOSHUA. Certainly, sir.

MESSERSCHMANN. That's all. Like Samson. With my eyes tight shut.

JOSHUA. Quite so, sir.

MESSERSCHMANN. And all at once there's a frightful uproar, a telephone ringing in the small hours. And that is the temple starting to crumble. Do you understand?

JOSHUA. No, sir.

MESSERSCHMANN. It doesn't matter. (*Moves to door* D. L.) Forget everything I've said. (*Stops and turns.*) And for supper, you remember—without butter. (*Exits* D. L.)

JOSHUA. (*Bowing.*) And without salt. (*Exits* D. R. *as* ——)

CURTAIN

SCENE: *The same. Dawn. The Ball is still in progress, but supper tables and chairs have been removed. When curtain rises, stage is empty.* ISABELLE *enters immediately* R. C., *crosses to steps, pauses, looks off* R. *then goes up on to rostrum, moves slowly up it, then exits* U. R. *As she exits,* MME. DESMORTES *wheels herself in* D. L. *Stops her chair* C., *looks after* ISABELLE *through her opera glasses. Music of a waltz commences off* L. CAPULET *enters excitedly* D. L., *crosses to* MME. DESMORTES.

CAPULET. Madam, madam! Everyone's searching the place for Isabelle. Her mother is out of her mind.

MME. DESMORTES. Why?

CAPULET. She has left her ring, the only valuable thing she has, wrapped up in a piece of paper on her dressing-table. Oh, madam, madam, we're all to blame. Mr. Hugo didn't love her.

MME. DESMORTES. You can cry later on, Capulet. (*Points off* U. R.) Look out there, down to the lake. (CAPULET *goes up on to rostrum, looks off* R.) Is there a white figure there?

CAPULET. There is, you're quite right. And it's Isabelle, it really is, it is really. Oh, dear, oh dear, unhappy girl. Oh, madam, she's leaning over the water. Oh, madam, madam, she has jumped. She'll be drowned, really she will, she will really.

MME. DESMORTES. No, she won't. There isn't enough water, and Hugo is down there. But she might quite well catch cold, and so might he. Run and get some blankets. (CAPULET *comes down steps, crosses below* MME. DESMORTES, *runs* U. R. *of conservatory, looks off* R.)

CAPULET. Mr. Hugo is there, you're quite right, he's there. He has plunged into the water. It's all right, I think, madam, it's all right. He'll save her.

MME. DESMORTES. It could hardly be less difficult.

CAPULET. He has picked her up in his arms, he has really, and they're coming glittering across the grass in an armor of moisture, madam, as you might say.

MME. DESMORTES. As I certainly wouldn't say. Stop talking nonsense, you stupid woman, and go at once and find some blankets.

(CAPULET *exits hurriedly* R. C. *She turns her chair, wheels herself*
D. L. C., *calls.*) Joshua! Joshua! Someone! Quickly! (JOSHUA
enters D. L., *moves to* L. *of chair.*)
JOSHUA. Madam?
MME. DESMORTES. I'm afraid we're having a little drama here this
evening, Joshua: heartbreak and attempted death by water. I'm
so sorry. Do go down to the kitchens and make some very hot
punch.
JOSHUA. Yes, madam. (*Moves to door* D. L., *then stops, turns.*)
Nothing serious, I hope?
MME. DESMORTES. Not at all. What a blessing you are, Joshua.
Do try never to break *your* heart, won't you?
JOSHUA. I handle it with as much care, madam, as if it was yours.
It's quite safe with me, madam.
MME. DESMORTES. The punch, Joshua.
JOSHUA. (*Bowing.*) Hot and very soon, madam. (*Exits* D. L. MME.
DESMORTES *wheels her chair* C. CAPULET *enters* R. C., *stands above*
MME. DESMORTES. HUGO, *carrying* ISABELLE, *enters* R. C. *They
each have a blanket over their shoulders.* HUGO *puts* ISABELLE *on
ground* L. *of chair, then eases* D. R.)
CAPULET. They're safe, they're safe, but they're wet.
MME. DESMORTES. Go and tell your friend that her daughter is
safe.
CAPULET. I will, I will. She was really out of her mind. (*Exits
D. L.*)
MME. DESMORTES. (*To* ISABELLE.) Are you cold, my dear?
ISABELLE. No, no, thanks; I'm not.
MME. DESMORTES. Joshua has gone to fetch you some punch.
Are you cold, Hugo?
HUGO. (*Stamping* U. *and* D. R. C.) Frozen, thank you, Aunt.
(*Music ceases.*)
MME. DESMORTES. Then let's make the most of being alone for a
few minutes. (ISABELLE *starts to rise.*) Stay as you are. (ISABELLE
subsides.) Sit down, Hugo. (HUGO *sits on ground* D. R., *his back
to* MME. DESMORTES *and* ISABELLE. *To* ISABELLE.) Now, look at
me, my dear. (ISABELLE *looks up at* MME. DESMORTES.) She's
even prettier with her hair down. Why do you ever wear it up?
ISABELLE. It's the usual way.
MME. DESMORTES. Is it also the usual way, at the first crossing of
love, to walk into a lake? You can swim, I imagine?

74

ISABELLE. Yes, I can swim.

MME. DESMORTES. You see how absurd you are.

HUGO. I suppose it was my fault. I asked her to pretend to drown herself for love of Frederic; but I cancelled the arrangement immediately afterwards. (*Rises, moves to* R. *of chair, shouts at* ISABELLE *across* MME. DESMORTES.) I simply don't know what she thought she was doing.

MME. DESMORTES. Why should you want to drown yourself?

ISABELLE. (*Half rising.*) For my own reasons.

HUGO. (*Shouting.*) It wasn't in our agreement. You were supposed to do what you were told.

ISABELLE. (*Shouting.*) My working day was over. You had already sent the butler to pay me; and I think I'm allowed to kill myself in my own free time, if I want to.

MME. DESMORTES. Certainly she is. (*Makes gesture to* HUGO *and* ISABELLE *to quiet them.* HUGO *sits cross-legged* R. *of chair.* ISABELLE *subsides.*) And it's very nearly morning, and Sunday morning, too. If a working man can't kill himself on a Sunday morning we may as well have the revolution at once.

"For pity, pretty eyes, surcease

To give me war and grant me peace."

You know you're a madman, don't you, Hugo?

HUGO. Yes, Aunt. (ISABELLE *leans against* L. *wheel of chair, cries quietly to herself.*)

MME. DESMORTES. He doesn't love you, my dear, and he'll never love you. He'll never love anyone, I think, if that's any consolation to you. He'll be amorous, perhaps, like a cat with a mouse, from time to time; but you're too delicate a mouse: he would eat you too soon, which he wouldn't like at all. And I'm going to tell you a splendid thing: he's not your sort of cat, either. (ISABELLE *stops crying.*) You think you're in love with him. You're not in love with him at all. Look at him. (*Points at* HUGO *with her stick.*) Look at this sulky Red Indian. Isn't he comic? (ISABELLE *looks at* HUGO.) You think he's handsome? Well, so he is, tolerably, when he's not thinking of anything. (ISABELLE *kneels* U. *She uses her stick to point out each feature.*) Clear eyes, straight nose, an interesting mouth. But let even the smallest of his wicked little thoughts creep into him—look at him now, for instance: we're annoying him: he wants to strangle us—and the change is quite terrifying. The nose is getting pinched, there's an angry little

75

crease tugging the mouth, the eyes are turning themselves into gimlets. And this chin. It suddenly makes him, wouldn't you say, into a fairly pretty but entirely wicked old woman? No one's altogether handsome who isn't altogether human.

HUGO. (*Rising, breaking* D. R.; *angrily*.) That's quite enough. If you want to analyze faces I'll go and send Frederic to you.

MME. DESMORTES. That's a very good idea. (HUGO *exits* D. R. ISABELLE *rises. She holds* ISABELLE'S *hand*.) No, my dear, it's the appearance of Hugo you love, not Hugo.

ISABELLE. (*Turning to face* L., *crying*.) Oh, it's terrible.

MME. DESMORTES. It .would be terrible if we only had one specimen; but fortunately we have two. (FREDERIC *enters* R. C. *She holds out hand to* FREDERIC.) Come here, my nephew. (FREDERIC *crosses to* R. *of* MME. DESMORTES, *holds her hand*.) You can look at him, Isabelle; it's the same picture as before. (ISABELLE *turns, then sits on ground* L. *of chair.* FREDERIC *sits on ground,* R. *of chair*.) Here is a young woman who was going to drown herself, and we can't get her to tell us why.

FREDERIC. (*To* ISABELLE.) I know why. I wish I could help you, but there's nothing I can do. There's something I want to tell you. When I left you just now I was being a coward for the last time. I followed Diana when she told me to. But when I caught her up I couldn't help telling her how wickedly she had treated you. And it's all over now: our engagement is broken off.

ISABELLE. Oh, no, no! Do you think it does any good for us both to be unhappy at once?

FREDERIC. I don't know, but I do know I couldn't love someone who could be so cruel.

MME. DESMORTES. Neither can Isabelle. She's beginning to see she could never love Hugo.

FREDERIC. I've finished with love altogether. I saw down to the sea-bed of a woman's heart.

ISABELLE. (*Smiling gently*.) The rocks that lie there, the sediments, the dead flowers, as your brother said.

FREDERIC. It's the worst plunge I ever took.

MME. DESMORTES. Come up to the surface again; there's still some dry land in places. (FREDERIC *and* ISABELLE *sigh, gaze out front.*)

FREDERIC. I'm going to find a desert island, out of the way of it all.

MME. DESMORTES. And so is Isabelle. Make sure that your desert islands aren't too far apart. You can have visiting days, hermit to hermit.

FREDERIC. I could have forgiven her for being unkind ——

ISABELLE. I saw from the first I had to take him as he was, and forgave him for that, but ——

FREDERIC. (*Kneeling up close to chair.*) I could have forgiven her for being hard, egotistical and hot-tempered ——

ISABELLE. (*Kneeling up close to chair.*) I could have forgiven him ——

MME. DESMORTES. The only thing you could never forgive them was not loving you. (*Puts her arms around their shoulders.*) We're terrible tailors. We cut the cloth, take no measurements, and when it doesn't fit we cry for help.

FREDERIC. And no one comes.

MME. DESMORTES. (*Withdrawing her arms.*) Or so we think. Not content with being blind we have to be deaf as well. We all go howling along together, never seeing or hearing who's beside us, and then we say we're in a wilderness. Luckily there are certain old women who have begun to see more clearly, just at the time, alas, when they're having to take to spectacles. (*Takes* ISABELLE'S *hand.*) Didn't you hear anything, young lady? This young gentleman called for help.

ISABELLE. How can I help him?

MME. DESMORTES. You can take him into the park and tell him why you feel so unhappy. (FREDERIC *rises, eases* R. C.) And he'll tell you why his life seems over. (ISABELLE *rises.*) Go along, my children, be as sad as you possibly can; (*Pushes* ISABELLE *gently toward* FREDERIC.) give her your arm, Frederic. (ISABELLE *moves to* FREDERIC.) You're quite alone in the world. No one is more hopeless than you are. (*Music of a waltz commences off* L. FREDERIC *leads* ISABELLE *to exit* R. C., *then they stop and turn.*)

FREDERIC. It's my own fault for being such a fool. I imagined women could be warm-hearted and have sincerity.

ISABELLE. And, of course, they can't. I imagined men could be honest and good and faithful.

FREDERIC. Faithful! We're faithful to ourselves, that's all. We dance the dance of the heart obstinately in front of a mirror. But I expected the dance to be with a partner.

ISABELLE. And there are no partners. (FREDERIC *and* ISABELLE *exit* R. C. MME. DESMORTES *looks after them a few moments.*)

77

MME. DESMORTES. Good. Those two only need another five minutes. Now for the others. (*Calls.*) Hugo! (HUGO *enters* D. R., *moves to* R. *of chair. Music ceases.*)

HUGO. Yes, Aunt?

MME. DESMORTES. That's as good as done. Now what have you decided?

HUGO. What do you want me to decide?

MME. DESMORTES. Either I'm a dense and myopic old woman, my dearest Hugo, or you're in love with Diana, and she with you and you have been since the first day you met.

HUGO. Absolutely ludicrous! And even if it were true, I'd rather die of jaundice, like your friend Palestrini you were talking about, than give her the pleasure of hearing me say so.

MME. DESMORTES. You can't die of jaundice—Palestrini's as well as you or I. Only last year he threw himself into a lagoon because he was in love with an Austrian swimming champion. (PATRICE *enters* R. C., *crosses above conservatory, goes to rostrum.*) She rescued him, and they have a baby. (HUGO *crosses to* L., *turns.*)

PATRICE. (*Crossing above* MME. DESMORTES *to* R.) Oh, there you are, I've been looking for you everywhere. (*Turns to face* L., *clicks his heels.*)

MME. DESMORTES. What does this madman want?

PATRICE. (*Crossing to* R. *of* HUGO.) Sir, as you will not give this young woman up of your own accord —— (*Slaps* HUGO's *face.* HUGO *grabs* PATRICE's *hand, pulls him sharply across front of himself to* L.)

HUGO. Go away, for Heaven's sake. (*Crosses above chair to* R. *of it.*) I won't have you making such a confounded nuisance of yourself.

PATRICE. Well, may you be forgiven.

HUGO. May I be forgiven—are you insulting me?

PATRICE. Yes, I am insulting you. You told me to insult you.

HUGO. Well, now I'm telling you to stop insulting me. Go away, for goodness sake.

PATRICE. (*Crossing to* L. *of* HUGO.) I demand satisfaction.

HUGO. (*Pushing* PATRICE U. C.) If you don't go I shall knock you down. (PATRICE *dodges above chair, seizes handle, and keeping chair between himself and* HUGO, *spins it in a complete circle as* HUGO *chases him round.*)

PATRICE. The arrangement was pistols—the arrangement was

pistols. (MME. DESMORTES strikes at HUGO and PATRICE with her stick. LADY INDIA enters D. L.)

LADY INDIA. (Moving to PATRICE; terrified.) Patrice. (PATRICE pushes chair R. C. HUGO moves to R. of PATRICE.)

PATRICE. Oh, my goodness, look, she's here. Do try to seem friendly. (Puts his arm around HUGO's shoulder. To LADY INDIA.) We were playing, my dear. We love playing together. A little early morning exercise, you know.

LADY INDIA. This is no time to be taking exercise, Patrice. (Crosses below PATRICE to L. of MME. DESMORTES.) Do you know what has happened? (MME. DESMORTES turns her chair to face LADY INDIA.) I've had a call from Paris. Messerschmann is out of his mind. He is selling in London, he is selling in New York, he is selling in Paris. He's ruining himself.

PATRICE. I don't believe it. I'll go and telephone to his brokers. (Exits hurriedly D. L. LADY INDIA follows him off. DIANA enters U. L., goes on to rostrum, stands at top of steps.)

DIANA. Have you heard the news? Within six hours my father will be a poor man.

HUGO. What are you going to do about it?

DIANA. (Moving to L. of HUGO.) Be poor. What do you expect me to do?

HUGO. Marry Frederic, who is rich.

DIANA. I don't want him. (Crosses below HUGO to R. of him.) And now he doesn't want me. Look at him, down there in the park with the little adventuress. She hasn't lost much time tonight. Was it you, Hugo, who taught her how to find a rich husband in one evening? You will have to teach me. I need one now.

HUGO. Let's be quite clear about this: it's a lesson that wouldn't help you in the least. (Moves toward exit R. C.)

MME. DESMORTES. Hugo, where are you going?

HUGO. (Stopping, turning.) I'm going to find Frederic. It's no good his thinking he can break the engagement now. Diana's ruined, and the honourable thing is to make her his wife.

DIANA. (Starting to cry.) But I don't want him.

HUGO. We can't help that. (Exits R. C. DIANA follows him off.)

MME. DESMORTES. (Wheeling herself to exit R. C.) Mille Tonnerres! He's going to mix everything up again. (Music for The Lancers commences off L. CAPULET enters D. L., runs across

79

to chair and swings it sharply round to face D. L. MOTHER *follows* CAPULET *on, stands* U. C.)

CAPULET. News! News! Extraordinary news. It is really. Really it is.

MME. DESMORTES. (*Wheeling herself* R. C.) I think we have heard it. (CAPULET *moves, stands above chair.*)

MOTHER. (*Moving to* L. *of chair.*) You've heard it? Now how could that possibly be? But news travels so fast these days. Here he is, to tell you himself. (MOTHER *eases a little* U. C. ROMAINVILLE *enters* D. L., *crosses to* L. *of chair. Wears a morning suit, white gloves, carries a bouquet.*)

ROMAINVILLE. My dear friend. In the first place, please excuse my clothes, but as dawn is about to break I changed into a morning coat: I felt it to be the correct wear for the present occasion. I'm going to give you some interesting news; my niece, dear friend, is not my niece—that was an entirely imaginary relationship spun from your nephew's fancy. But she is about to become even more nearly related. After extremely careful thought, I've decided to marry her. (CAPULET *eases to* R. *of* MOTHER. DIANA *enters* D. R., *stands with back to audience.*)

MME. DESMORTES. My good man, I would be the first to congratulate you, (*Turns her chair to face* R.) but I have an idea that you're too late.

ROMAINVILLE. Too late? What can you mean? It's five o'clock in the morning. (ISABELLE *and* FREDERIC, *their arms around one another, enter* R. C., *move to* R. *of* MME. DESMORTES. ISABELLE *stands above* FREDERIC. JOSHUA *enters* D. L., *stands below door. Carries a tray with two glasses of punch on it.* LADY INDIA *follows* JOSHUA *on, goes on to rostrum, stands at top of steps, leaning on post* R. *of them, and looking off* R.)

MME. DESMORTES. (*To* ISABELLE *and* FREDERIC.) Well, my children, what news have you for us? Have you altered the fit of the coat?

ISABELLE. There wasn't any need to alter it. It fitted perfectly.

FREDERIC. Aunt, I must have been out of my mind. (*Turns to* DIANA.) I don't love you any more, Diana; do forgive me.

ISABELLE. Why couldn't I have known it from the first? It was Frederic, just as you said. (FREDERIC *and* ISABELLE *embrace and kiss.*)

80

MOTHER. } (Together.) { Oh, how splendid.
CAPULET. }   { She's in love with Frederic.
(MOTHER *moves to* ISABELLE *and kisses her.* FREDERIC *kisses*
MOTHER. MME. DESMORTES *turns her chair to face* ROMAINVILLE.)
MME. DESMORTES. Romainville, you'll have to get some other
niece. This is the one you have to give away. (MOTHER *moves to*
R. *of* CAPULET.)
ROMAINVILLE. It's appalling! (*Sits on steps at* R. *end of them.*)
I had just got used to the idea.
MME. DESMORTES. Joshua, give him some of the punch. (JOSHUA
moves to ROMAINVILLE, *who takes glass of punch from tray.*
JOSHUA *then returns* D. L.) But where is Hugo? Someone go and
find him at once. He has made this girl unhappy for quite long
enough. (DIANA *crosses to* R. *of* MME. DESMORTES. *To* DIANA.)
Don't be too dismayed; he loves you, he told me so.
LADY INDIA. Why, look. He's down there in the park, escaping.
MME. DESMORTES. Escaping? Joshua, catch him before he goes,
and bring him here. (JOSHUA *crosses, exits* D. R. *To* DIANA.) He's
a thoroughly crack-brained boy, but he knows he's cornered; he's
certain to come back.
DIANA. But suppose he doesn't love me?
MME. DESMORTES. Impossible. Everything has to end happily, it's
only decent. Besides here he is. (DIANA *crosses, stands below exit*
D. R. CAPULET *pushes* MME. DESMORTES *and sets chair* D. R. *to*
face D. R. *exit.* MOTHER *moves, stands* U. R. *of* CAPULET. FREDERIC
and ISABELLE *turn and face* R.) Well, Hugo? (*Everyone looks*
toward exit D. R. *through which* HUGO *should enter. A pause, then*
JOSHUA *enters* D. R. *Carries a note.*)
FREDERIC. (*Turning to face audience.*) I knew he wouldn't come.
JOSHUA. (*Standing* R. *of* MME. DESMORTES.) Mr. Hugo has given
me this note for you, madam.
MME. DESMORTES. Read it aloud, Joshua.
JOSHUA. (*Reading.*) "Dear Aunt, for reasons which you all
know, I'm not able to appear among you to take part in the
general rejoicing. There's nothing I've ever regretted more. But
now Diana is poor I know I love her." (DIANA *moves, kneels* D. R.
of MME. DESMORTES.) "Nothing will separate us again. I shall
marry her. Tell her to look for me in the park."
MME. DESMORTES. (*To* DIANA.) Off you go.
DIANA. (*Rising, happily.*) Yes, I will. (*Kisses* FREDERIC, *then turns,*

kisses MME. DESMORTÈS.) Oh, Hugo! Hugo! (*Exits quickly* U. R. *Music of The Lancers fades out and is replaced by that of a polka.* JOSHUA *eases* U. R. C. MESSERSCHMANN *enters* D. L. *Wears an overcoat and hat too small for him, carries a very small attaché case.* CAPULET *turns chair to face* L. *and stands* R. *of it.* MESSES-SCHMANN *crosses to* L. *of* MME. DESMORTES.)

MME. DESMORTES. What's this, will someone tell me?

MESSERSCHMANN. It is I, madam. I've come to say good-bye. (*Kisses* MME. DESMORTES' *hand.*)

MME. DESMORTES. But the suitcase, the hat, the coat?

MESSERSCHMANN. (*Shaking hands with* CAPULET.) I borrowed them from your butler. (*Shakes hands with* FREDERIC.) I've nothing of my own to put on. (*Shakes hands with* ISABELLE.) I'm ruined. (*Shakes hands with* MOTHER.) I shall return them in a few years' time. (*Crosses to* ROMAINVILLE. ROMAINVILLE *rises. Shakes hands with* ROMAINVILLE.) I'm going back to Cracow on foot, (*Moves* D. C.) to start a small tailoring business.

LADY INDIA. (*Running to* L. *of* MESSERSCHMANN, *putting her arms around him.*) Oh, my darling boy, what a great, great man you are after all. (JOSHUA *crosses to* ROMAINVILLE, *takes his glass, then exits* D. L.) You must love me so much, so beautifully. It was for me, wasn't it, that you ruined yourself?

MESSERSCHMANN. (*Releasing himself from* LADY INDIA, *shaking hands with her.*) Good-bye. (*Crosses below* LADY INDIA *to* L. C.)

LADY INDIA. I'll follow you—(*Moves to* R. *of* MESSERSCHMANN.) barefooted to the bottom of the Steppes of Siberia. (*Kneels* R. *of* MESSERSCHMANN. CAPULET *wheels* MME. DESMORTES *to* R. *of* LADY INDIA.)

MME. DESMORTES. She gets so muddled.

LADY INDIA. I'll cook for you, my darling, in your dark, dingy igloo, ever your faithful squaw.

MME. DESMORTES. She hasn't even a working idea of geography. (*The bangs and cracks of exploding fireworks are heard off. Music fades out.* MESSERSCHMANN *moves* D. L. PATRICE *enters* D. L., *runs across stage, exits* R. C.)

PATRICE. (*As he crosses.*) There they go! They've started.

LADY INDIA. (*Turning on her knees to* MME. DESMORTES.) What is it? The fire from heaven already? (FREDERIC *takes* ISABELLE'S *hand, leads her up steps on to rostrum, moves up it, crosses above conservatory, leads her off* U. R.)

82

MME. DESMORTES. No. We haven't deserved that, not quite, not yet. It's my firework display, which all the upset tonight has made a little late. (LADY INDIA *rises, exits* R. C. CAPULET *turns chair to face* R.) Come along, come and watch: the gardener will be so disappointed if we don't. It will feel rather odd, in broad daylight. We shall hardly be able to see them. (CAPULET *wheels* MME. DESMORTES *off* R. C. ROMAINVILLE *and* MOTHER *follow them off.* MESSERSCHMANN *moves toward exit* R. C. *As he does so,* JOSHUA. *enters* D. L. *Carries telegram. Noise of fireworks ceases.*) JOSHUA. (*As he enters.*) Sir, sir, sir! A telegram for you, sir. (MESSERSCHMANN *stops, turns.* JOSHUA *moves to* L. *of him, hands him telegram.*)

MESSERSCHMANN. (*Opening telegram.*) Who is still sufficiently interested in me to send me a telegram? A letter would have done just as well. (*Reads telegram, then sighs.*) How funny it all is.

JOSHUA. (*Compassionately.*) All over, sir, is it? If you should still need anything, sir—I've got a small amount in the savings-bank.

MESSERSCHMANN. What? No, thank you. It's not so easy to ruin yourself as you'd think. It was believed to be a manoeuvre on the stock exchange. They bought everything, and now I'm twice as rich as I was before. (*Tears up telegram.*) But I do beg of you: don't let anyone know.

JOSHUA. I must say, I'm very happy for you, sir. I should have felt very sad, sir, not to have brought you your breakfast. (*Takes up his butler's stance.*) Without butter?

MESSERSCHMANN. Yes, my friend. But this morning as a special celebration, you may add a little salt. (*Puts his finger to his lips, crosses below* JOSHUA *to* L., *picks up his case.*)

JOSHUA. Ah, it's a happy day for me, sir, to see you taking such a pleasure in life again. (MESSERSCHMANN *and* JOSHUA *exit* D. L. *The bangs and cracks of fireworks are heard off, rocket effects become visible through backcloth. Cast fill the stage, stand for a few moments with their backs to audience gazing at fireworks, then turn and take their bows as ——*)

CURTAIN FALLS

PROPERTY LIST

Act I—Scene 1

On stage:
Wicker rocking couch. *On it:*
   cushions

Off stage:
Suitcase (Isabelle)
Suitcase (Mother)
Handkerchief (Capulet)
Wheel-chair with ebony stick in
   carrier (Mme. Desmortes)
Cup and ball (Double)

Personal:
Hugo: Cup and ball
Patrice: Monocle
Romainville: Spectacles, butter-
   fly net, shooting-stick
Mme. Desmortes: Small basket.
   In it: fan, handkerchief, snuff-
   box, opera glasses
Capulet: Parasol
Lady India: Parasol

Act I—Scene 2

Strike:
Couch
Set:
Step-ladder
Chair R. C.
Champagne box L. C.
Lanterns with drape

Off stage:

Tool-box (Joshua)
List of guests (Capulet)

Personal:
Hugo: Cigar in cigar case, cigar
   holder, matches or lighter, watch
Romainville: matches
Capulet: boa
Mme. Desmortes: basket as before

Act II

Set:
Flower bed
Two chairs

Off stage:
Key (Joshua)
Fan (Capulet)

Personal:
Romainville: spectacles
Patrice: gloves
Hugo: cigar and matches
Mme. Desmortes: basket as before

Act III—Scene 1

Strike:
Trellis
Two chairs
Flower bed

Set:
Table U. C. *On it:* champagne
   in bottle, champagne glasses,
   fruit, sweets, dressing, etc.

Table R. C. *On it:* fruit, dressing,
    etc.
Table D. R. *On it:* ash-tray, dress-
    ing, etc.
White cloths on all three tables
Six chairs

Personal:
Messerschmann: bundles of bank
    notes
Hugo: lighted cigar

ACT III—SCENE 2

Strike:
All furniture and debris

Off stage:
Blanket (Hugo)
Blanket (Isabelle)
Note (Joshua)
Bouquet (Romainville)

Tray. *On it:* two glasses of punch
    (Joshua)
Small attaché case
    (Messerschmann)
Telegram (Joshua)

Personal:
Mme. Desmortes: basket as before

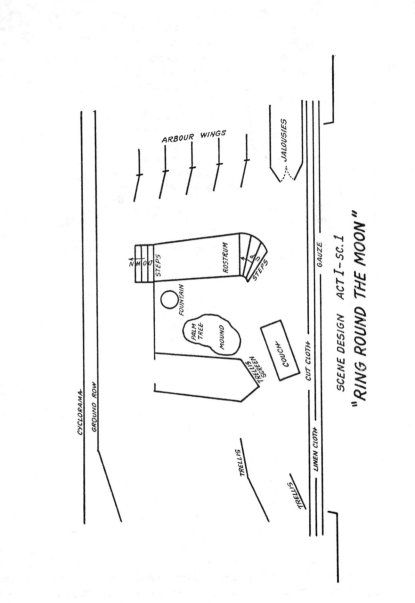

SCENE DESIGN ACT I - SC. 1
"RING ROUND THE MOON"

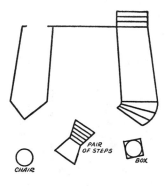

ACT I - SCENE 2

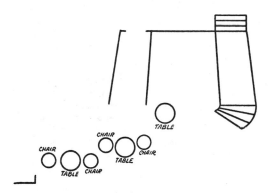

ACT III - SCENE 1

SCENE DESIGNS

"RING ROUND THE MOON"

NEW PLAYS

- **A QUESTION OF MERCY by David Rabe.** The Obie Award-winning playwright probes the sensitive and controversial issue of doctor-assisted suicide in the age of AIDS in this poignant drama. *"There are many devastating ironies in Mr. Rabe's beautifully considered, piercingly clear-eyed work ... " –The NY Times.* *"With unsettling candor and disturbing insight, the play arouses pity and understanding of a troubling subject ... Rabe's provocative tale is an affirmation of dignity that rings clear and true." –Variety.* [6M, 1W] ISBN: 0-8222-1643-4

- **A DOLL'S HOUSE by Henrik Ibsen, adapted by Frank McGuinness. Winner of the 1997 Tony Award for best revival.** *"New, raw, gut-twisting and gripping. Easily the hottest drama this season." –USA Today.* *"Bold, brilliant and alive." –The Wall Street Journal.* *"A thunderclap of an evening that takes your breath away." –Time.* *"The stuff of Broadway legend." –Associated Press.* [4M, 4W, 2 boys] ISBN: 0-8222-1636-1

- **THE WAITING ROOM by Lisa Loomer.** Three women from different centuries meet in a doctor's waiting room in this dark comedy about the timeless quest for beauty -- and its cost. *"... THE WAITING ROOM ... is a bold, risky melange of conflicting elements that is ... terrifically moving ... There's no resisting the fierce emotional pull of the play." – The NY Times.* *"... one of the high points of this year's Off-Broadway season ... THE WAITING ROOM is well worth a visit." –Back Stage.* [7M, 4W, flexible casting] ISBN: 0-8222-1594-2

- **MR. PETERS' CONNECTIONS by Arthur Miller.** Mr. Miller describes the protagonist as existing in a dream-like state when the mind is "freed to roam from real memories to conjectures, from trivialities to tragic insights, from terror of death to glorying in one's being alive." With this memory play, the Tony Award and Pulitzer Prize-winner reaffirms his stature as the world's foremost dramatist. *" ... a cross between Joycean stream-of-consciousness and Strindberg's dream plays, sweetened with a dose of William Saroyan's philosophical whimsy ... CONNECTIONS is most intriguing ... Miller scholars will surely find many connections of their own to make between this work and the author's earlier plays." –The NY Times.* [5M, 3W] ISBN: 0-8222-1687-6

- **THE STEWARD OF CHRISTENDOM by Sebastian Barry.** A freely imagined portrait of the author's great-grandfather, the last Chief Superintendent of the Dublin Metropolitan Police. *"MAGNIFICENT ... the cool, elegiac eye of James Joyce's THE DEAD; the bleak absurdity of Samuel Beckett's lost, primal characters; the cosmic anger of KING LEAR ..." –The NY Times.* *"Sebastian Barry's compassionate imaging of an ancestor he never knew is among the most poignant onstage displays of humanity in recent memory." –Variety.* [5M, 4W] ISBN: 0-8222-1609-4

- **SYMPATHETIC MAGIC by Lanford Wilson. Winner of the 1997 Obie for best play.** The mysteries of the universe, and of human and artistic creation, are explored in this award-winning play. *"Lanford Wilson's idiosyncratic SYMPATHETIC MAGIC is his BEST PLAY YET ... the rare play you WANT ... chock-full of ideas, incidents, witty or poetic lines, scientific and philosophical argument ... you'll find your intellectual faculties racing." – New York Magazine.* *"The script is like a fully notated score, next to which most new plays are cursory lead sheets." –The Village Voice.* [5M, 3W] ISBN: 0-8222-1630-2

DRAMATISTS PLAY SERVICE, INC.
440 Park Avenue South, New York, NY 10016 212-683-8960 Fax 212-213-1539
postmaster@dramatists.com www.dramatists.com